ASTROLAND
CYCLONE
ELDORADO
ELDORADO
WONDER
THRILLS
SPOOKARAMA
HOME MADE
PIZZA

THE
AMERICAN
Roller
Coaster

SCOTT RUTHERFORD

MBI Publishing Company

Dedication

This book is dedicated with love to my dad, Jesse. He may be gone now, but I'm glad he was there to hold on to me during that all-important First Ride. In a sense, I suspect he still watches over me, even though I can now make it on my own. And with equal sentiment and affection, this is for my courageous mom, Phyllis. I'm eternally grateful to her for braving that initial ride, and for unconditionally sticking by me through the countless others life has thrown my way.—*Scott Rutherford*

Acknowledgments

After seemingly endless months of work, research, traveling and, of course, coaster riding, this book is finally completed. Compiling a history of anything is a monumental undertaking, and delving into the past is always a learning experience, regardless of how much you may think you know about a particular subject.

First, a thanks must go to Andover Junction Publications' book editor and art director Mike Schafer for his innate knowledge of the subject matter, exemplary layout skills, and infinite patience in bringing this project to fruition. It was long and complicated journey, but hopefully the product you are holding speaks for itself.

Endless thanks as well must go to Tom Rebbie of Philadelphia Toboggan Coasters for allowing me access the PTC collection of priceless roller coaster artifacts. Similarly, I am indebted to the many amusement parks who shared their resources and to my friends and fellow coaster fans for their support and contributions: Edward Kirkland, Gary Slade (*Amusement Today*), Terry Lind, B. Derek Shaw, Scott Shermeyer, George Siessel, Otto P. Dobnick, John Hunt, Frank and Teresa Purtiman of Intraxx, Charlie Jacques, David Johnson, Bill Figie, Justin Garvanovic, Chuck Davis, Doug Garner, Mike Boodley of Great Coasters International, Lee O. Bush and Richard Hershey of Amusement Park Books, and any others I've not mentioned.

In closing, I would also like to thank Steve Esposito at Andover Junction Publications, the producer of this book, as well as the good people at MBI Publishing, this book's publisher, for giving me the chance to write about a subject that is very dear to my heart.

—*Scott Rutherford*

First published in 2000 by MBI Publishing Company, 729 Prospect Avenue, PO Box 1, Osceola, WI 54020-0001 USA

© Andover Junction Publications, 2000.

Edited by Mike Schafer; book design and layout by Mike Schafer and Maureene Gulbrandsen, Andover Junction Publications, Blairstown, New Jersey, and Lee, Illinois.

Library of Congress Cataloging-in-Publication Data available
ISBN 0-7603-0689-3

Front cover: Passengers enjoy a spin on the spunky *Tornado* coaster at Adventureland Park near Des Moines, Iowa, in 1982. *Mike Schafer*
End sheets: A 1978 snapshot of the *Rocket* at Ocean View Park in Norfolk, Virginia. *Scott Rutherford collection*
Frontispiece: Coaster riders are frozen in time on bas relief metalwork adorning the railings of the ramps leading to and from the boarding station of the *Cyclone* coaster at Lakeside Park, Denver, Colorado. *Mike Schafer*

Title page: America's best-known roller coaster, the *Cyclone*, looms over the crowds at New York's Coney Island on a late summer afternoon in 1985. *Otto P. Dobnick*
Contents page: Signage invites potential riders to brave the coaster of their choice: the *Little Dipper*, Kennywood Park, West Mifflin, Pennsylvania; *Wild Chipmunk,* Lakeside Park, Denver, Colorado; *The Racer*, Paramount's Kings Island, Kings Island, Ohio; *Racer*, Kennywood Park; *Z-Force*, Six Flags Great America, Gurnee, Illinois; *Thunderbolt*, Six Flags New England, Agawam, Massachusetts. The Racer *photo by David P. Oroszi;* Z-Force, *Otto P. Dobnick; all others, Mike Schafer*
Foreword pages: A front-seat view aboard a train about to swoop through the vertical loop of the splendid *Superdooperlooper* at Hersheypark, Pennsylvania. *Mike Schafer*
Introduction, page 8: Riders savor a plunge on the *Shooting Star* at Cincinnati's Coney Island in May 1970. This was the first coaster ridden by this book's author. *David P. Oroszi.*
Introduction, page 9: A tense Bobby Scheer of Blairstown, New Jersey, chaperones Anna Mercurio and Ashley Pennell on their first coaster ride, aboard the *Hercules* at Dorney Park, Allentown, Pennsylvania, in the summer of 1999. *Dorney Park photo, courtesy Bob Scheer*
Glossary page: A stored train in the station of the celebrated *Wildcat* coaster at the now-defunct Idora Park, Youngstown, Ohio, in 1983. *Mike Schafer*
Back cover photos (clockwise from top): One of America's earliest modern looping coasters, the *Demon* (built as the *Turn of the Century* in 1976 and modified in 1980), at Great America near Chicago, remains a favorite even though larger loopers have since debuted at this park. *Otto P. Dobnick*

Denver's famous *Cyclone* coaster lives in a world of Art Deco at Lakeside Park.

Some coasters have survived only in postcard form, such as this of the late lamented *Tornado* at New York's Coney Island. *Collection of Otto P. Dobnick*

Edited and designed by Mike Schafer

Printed in China

Contents

Foreword

By the time I landed on this planet in 1949, my hometown, Rockford, Illinois, had become completely devoid of coasters. The little Figure-8 coaster at Harlem Park had long since vanished, and the wonderful John Miller-designed *Jack Rabbit* at Central Park—where my folks and uncle used to hang out in the 1930s—had been razed. After World War II, Rockford had a small new park known as Kiddieland, aimed primarily at us baby-boomers. It had the obligatory carousel, Ferris wheel, pony rides, and miniature train, but there was no roller coaster.

Regardless, by the early 1950s I had an intense interest both in roller coasters and railroads. Why roller coasters in a city void of them (we had plenty of railroads, and Kiddieland did have its miniature train)? Well, I had learned of coasters through the new television medium and had become completely entranced by them. Even though I had never seen a real coaster, I built models of them with anything I could find: Tinkertoys, Erector sets, cardboard . . . you name it.

Finally a miracle happened: Kiddieland opened its new *Little Dipper* in the late 1950s, an all-steel kid-size coaster manufactured by Herschel. I was in heaven! Still, I craved to ride a real live towering wooden coaster. Alas, that would not happen until I was 18, in 1967.

That year, I finally made my first pilgrimage to the America's greatest coaster mecca, Riverview Park in Chicago. I had spent much of my early teen years listening to WLS Radio (AM 8.90) broadcast from nearby Chicago, and I had heard Riverview commercials hundreds of times. In May 1967, four of us high-school seniors ventured to the revered park, where we first boarded the *Comet,* and I thus lost my wood coaster virginity. Right after, we rode what was then one of America's ultimate roller coasters, the famed *Bobs.* I was blown away.

My interest in coasters rebounded, but it wasn't until 1978 that I discovered there were other folks around who had this uncanny fascination in coasters. That was the year I discovered the newly formed American Coaster Enthusiasts. Coasterwise, my life hasn't been the same since, and it's been a wonderful trip.

That said, I wish Scott's book had been around 45 years ago! Here is a book that would have answered countless questions about coasters that I had as a kid and at the same time provided some enticing entertainment. But it's here now, and I trust that *The American Roller Coaster* will provide answers and entertainment to new generations of fans of those marvelous machines we all know, love, and ride.

—*Mike Schafer*
Past Publications Director/American Coaster Enthusiasts

Introduction

During a family vacation in the summer of 1970 I experienced my very first major roller coaster. The event took place aboard a tricky wooden thriller called the *Shooting Star* at Cincinnati's Coney Island. It happened just before that grand old park perched on the banks of the Ohio River was closed and its rides dismantled.

Fate Rides a Shooting Star

On the way to Coney, I'd overheard the grownups bragging about how the *Shooting Star* was a "real legend" and "one of the best old wooden coasters still around." They agreed that I was finally ready for it. Ready for what, I wondered with undeclared trepidation.

I suddenly understood, once I finally stood before that 1930s classic. Clutching a single ride ticket, I stared up in silent wonder at a towering mountain of white-washed wood. At the tender age of nine, I had no real point of reference as to what I should expect, but from the context of the adults' earlier conversation, I gathered that riding this thundering beast was some traditional rite of passage for a young boy. It was just something you had to do.

Of course, it was a well-known fact that I openly harbored an unusual love of carnival rides. I suppose that because of my obsession with all things amusement park–related, I was considered quite fearless. Or strange. Perhaps both. And though I'd been raised in a small Appalachian mountain town and had never ridden a real wooden roller coaster, I still knew the basic premise of what I was in for. "It's a real fast train ride," my dad had said during a brief explanation of what the ride would involve. As it turned out, I was completely unprepared for the outrageous and ultimately life-altering ordeal awaiting me.

I remember being ushered up a long wooden ramp and then snugly wedged into the coaster's front seat between my Dad and a family friend. The very front offers the best view, I was promptly informed. With a definitive click, an attendant lowered a thin iron bar across our laps. I watched with fascination as he then used his weight to pull a long wooden lever anchored to the floor. The bright red train began to move, rumbling slowly down and out of the station. As we gained speed and raced to catch up to an oily, moving chain, I sensed an infectious air of excitement spreading among the other passengers. It seemed as if most everyone else was looking forward to whatever was about to happen.

Climbing that first hill, I vividly recall closing my eyes and inhaling the earthy scent of hot grease and sunshine on dried wood. Above the metallic clanking of the lift, muted giggles and squeals from other riders filled the late-summer air.

I stole a quick glance over my shoulder to check on my Mom, who was seated directly behind us with another family friend. Something was wrong. She didn't share the others' elation at all. Instead, a grimace of sheer terror shadowed her pretty face. Clutching her purse, she appeared regretful. This was her first coaster ride as well, and I was puzzled, since everyone else appeared expectant. What did she know that I didn't?

Before I had time to ask my Dad about this turn of events, we reached the crest of that impossibly tall first hill, made a left turn—and my view of the world and what I considered reality were irrevocably altered.

A gut-wrenching nose dive straight to the ground forcefully ripped the breath from my lungs. I swiftly grasped the rationale behind my mother's apprehension. I felt as if I'd been strapped to a searing bolt of wicked lightning that was intent on tossing me out of that rocketing car. Up, down, up, down. It seemed to go on forever. The sense of speed was greatly magnified by the close proximity of wooden beams flashing mere inches past my head.

Screeching around a quick turnaround, I was slammed into our family friend and noticed August sunlight sparkling on the surface of the nearby Ohio. But the slow-moving water was instantly forgotten when the floor of the car was again yanked away. We were soaring once more, this time over a series of smaller yet more violent hills, furiously racing back to the place where it had all begun.

At one moment I was pinned to the cushioned seat by an astonishing degree of gravity, while at other times I was actually floating, flying, screaming. My sun-bleached blond hair whipped around my eyes as if we'd been swept into a cyclone. During a particularly steep and unexpected plunge, the howling wind took hold and wrenched me skyward. I vaguely recall my Dad laughing with glee and wrapping a protective arm around my skinny shoulders to prevent his only son from taking flight and leaving the family.

It was unbelievably loud, rattling, terrifying; an emotional episode the likes of which I had never before experienced. But as the speeding train neared the end of its course, my fear rapidly melted into something else altogether—a sense that it was O.K. to howl with delight like everyone else, to let go, to have fun. Once you got the hang of it, the *Shooting Star* didn't seem so bad after all.

Just as I had come to this realization, that deceptive and fiendish coaster delivered a totally unforeseen kick in the pants. The finale was the ride's best-kept secret to those who had never ridden before. A reckless right turn sent our train sailing over a sharp drop and into the dank, cave-like coolness of a hidden tunneled spiral. It was roaring madness at breakneck speed, noisy and more frenzied than any nightmare I could remember.

And just as abruptly, we exploded back into the daylight and began to slow through a gentle curve leading into the main station house. The brakes took hold, and I managed to relax my death grip on the lap bar. When the train of cheering, laughing riders finally stopped, my Dad helped me and then my Mom from our seats, and we all wobbled down the exit ramp to the relative sanity of the bustling midway.

"Well," my dad asked with an eager grin, "what did you think?"

With my shaking hands jammed into the pockets of my worn Levi's, I glanced at my mom standing nearby and tried to form a coherent response. She was still, windblown, and silent. Her purse seemed strangely void of half its contents.

I stood there trying to process what had just happened. Time seemed to have stopped. I knew I'd endured and survived something far removed from what mere words could possibly describe. It had been almost spiritual in nature, but impossible to understand unless experienced firsthand. That single ride had been shocking, seemingly brutal, yet more intense and empowering than anything I'd ever done. I was instantly aware that a rare and pivotal moment in my young life had just occurred. On some primal level, I knew with complete and utter certainty that something inside me had changed, that the ramifications of that fantastic adventure had affected me more than I could ever imagine. At the time, I had no idea how the simple encounter with my first wooden roller coaster would influence and shape the course of my life and career so drastically. Looking back now, though, it's quite clear. It was simply fate.

Because of my prolonged silence and distant stare, my Dad presumed that I had been completely traumatized and was bordering on meltdown. But then I looked up at him, my eyes brimming with tears; and I grinned and, in my trembling, squeaky nine-year-old voice, said, "Let's do it again."

That tumultuous flight aboard a legend called the *Shooting Star* ignited my longtime love affair with the roller coaster. And to this very day, my passion for these remarkable machines burns brightly still.

—*Scott Rutherford*
Charlotte, North Carolina

Humble Beginnings

America Goes Coasting: 1800s–1920

Lake and Dip the D
North Side, F

DIP-THE-DIP, WEST VIEW PARK, PITTSBURGH

The roller coaster plays prominent in this early twentieth century scene of West View Park on the north side of Pittsburgh, Pennsylvania. Folks wearing their Sunday attire stroll along the lake whose backdrop is the white wooden structure of the *Dip-the-Dip*, a ride with gentle hills and valleys. The roller coaster and the amusement park were coming of age. In a few years, this coaster would be rebuilt with steeper drops to please thrill-seekers, and it would last almost to the 1980s when this wonderful park succumbed to the times. *Mike Schafer collection*

The actual origin of the modern roller coaster has been debated among amusement park historians and coaster enthusiasts for decades. Available records indicate that the original concept of building gravity-powered pleasure devices can be traced back to wintertime recreation in St. Petersburg and other Russian cities during the 1400s. But these "Russian Mountains," as they were called, were a far cry from the high-tech thrillers we enjoy today. They were instead long, narrow ice slides built atop a sloping wooden framework. During the lengthy Russian winters, eager thrillseekers carried sleds or toboggans (sometimes fashioned from mere blocks of

West View Park,
urgh, Pa.

Generally regarded as America's
first roller coaster (and second
railroad), the Summit Hill-Mauch
Chunk Railroad—later known as
the Mauch Chunk Switch Back
Railway—was built in 1827 to haul
coal down from mountaintop mines
to the Lehigh River at Mauch
Chunk, Pennsylvania. Eventually
the railroad also began hauling
passengers, a carload of which is
shown being hoisted to the summit
of Mount Pisgah from Mauch
Chunk, much like a present-day
roller coaster train is lifted to start
its run. *Chuck Graver collection
Switch Back Gravity Railroad
Foundation*

ice) to the tops of these primitive structures. They
were then rewarded with a brisk and somewhat harrowing ride to the bottom of the run. As the years
passed, the slides became larger and more elaborate
(and more dangerous), developing into a very popular
pastime. The activity was reported to have been a
favorite of Russian aristocrats.

By the 1700s, the technology had advanced to the
point where the activity was more than a cold-weather
pastime. The sleds had been fitted with wheels and
carried riders down undulating wooden ramps from
the lofty height of six stories. The concept spread, and
even today "Russian Mountains" is a common term
for the roller coaster in several languages.

In the early 1800s, a more sophisticated version of
the wood-track, steel-wheeled ride appeared in pleasure gardens around France. These ornate attractions,
referred to, among other things, as *Les Montagnes
Russes* (again, *Russian Mountains*), were far from
technologically perfect; but they were enormously
popular with the daring French. Numerous incarnations sprang up and became cultural sensations. In
1817, a dual-track ride called the *Aerial Walks*
opened in Paris' Beaujon Gardens. This elegantly

crafted attraction reportedly later became the first
pleasure railway using a cable system to raise the passenger vehicles.

With all this action happening in Europe, it was only
a matter of time before the rides caught the eye of
inventors across the Atlantic.

The Roller Coaster Comes to America

Concerning North America's first roller coaster,
there again exists a series of debates. Some say the
honor belongs to Josiah White, a coal-mining entre-
preneur who turned an 1827-built coal transport railroad located in Mauch Chunk (now Jim Thorpe),
Pennsylvania, into a tourist attraction. Originally called
the Summit Hill-Mauch Chunk Railroad, it featured
mules hauling trains of empty mine cars along rails
from Mauch Chunk to mines at the top of Summit
Hill. Once there, the vehicles were loaded with coal
and allowed to roll back down the winding mountain
path—with the mules riding in their own cars—to be
unloaded. By 1829, a growing number of tourists
were allowed to take the place of the coal in the after-
noons for the rather hefty charge of 50 cents a head.

White realized he was on to something with both the coal business and the tourist trade, but the single-track operation was becoming crowded due to the demand for the rich anthracite coal buried in the mountains. By 1845, the SH-MCRR was overhauled and expanded. It now consisted of a complete loop, beginning with a pair of parallel tracks starting in Mauch Chunk and climbing steeply up a 2,322-foot incline to the top of Mount Pisgah. The ascent was accomplished by using a steam-driven cable system to pull a pair of opposing transport cars (one at the top, one at the bottom, passing at the halfway point). After completing the ascent, the passenger/coal car was released to coast six miles to the base of Mount Jefferson. There it was raised by another incline plane to the top of that peak, only to begin the climactic and reportedly harrowing downhill trip back to Mauch Chunk. The entire circuit was 18 miles long.

By the 1870s the railway had been renamed Mauch Chunk-Summit Hill & Switch Back Railroad. The "switchback" term referred to the reverse in direction that cars had to make during the descent. A car would coast into an inclined dead-end "tail" track, the track switched behind it, and then the car would

begin rolling in the opposite direction and enter the diverging route to continue downhill. This aspect of operation plays into the first "true" roller coaster—that is, a gravity ride built expressly for pleasure—that will be covered shortly.

In 1872, a nearby tunnel was completed on a regular steam railroad, allowing the coal to be transported in a more conventional manner and rendering the loop/incline/switchback system redundant. The owners saw this as an advantage and transformed the whole operation into a tourist attraction.

The MC-SHSB was a sensation, drawing enormous numbers of tourists for the excursion. With a restaurant, hotel, and various activities available atop Mount

SWITCHBACK, FOLKESTONE.

Jefferson, there was plenty to do besides admire the stunning view of the surrounding mountains. By 1874, word had spread of this most unusual expedition, and train service between metropolitan New York City and the Mauch Chunk area was implemented. It has been reported that 35,000 people rode the Mauch Chunk-Summit Hill Switch Back Railroad each year.

In 1912 the operation became known as the Mauch Chunk Switch Back Railway. Due to a variety of circumstances, including the dark specter of the Great Depression, the attraction closed in 1937. Some—including today's Switch Back Gravity Railroad Foundation—say the Mauch Chunk Switch Back Railway was North America's first roller coaster while others say it was also the first railroad in North America (it was the second). In any case, it was a monumental engineering accomplishment. It featured numerous concepts that would later manifest themselves in the evolving world of roller coasters, most notably its lift system, anti-rollback devices on the steep climbs, and—most of all—its gravity-powered operation. The Switch Back's properties very likely influenced inventors such as La Marcus Thompson in the development of his *Switch Back Railway* coaster and enormously popular *Scenic Railways*.

Today, remains of the Switch Back Railway can still be found in the woods around Jim Thorpe, where the local historical society features a working model of the Switch Back. The paths over which speeding excursion cars once ran are now used by hikers and other outdoor enthusiasts.

The First True American Roller Coaster

Most historians, backed up by available records, concur that the first authentic American roller coaster structure—that is, one built expressly for entertainment purposes—appeared at New York's Coney Island in 1884. Designed by La Marcus Thompson, it was called none other than the *Switch Back Railway*. The name and the pseudo switchback-track format underscore the belief that Thompson had visited— and was inspired by—the Mauch Chunk operation.

This meager ride was approximately 600 feet long and stood about 50 feet tall. Riders paid 5 cents each to climb aboard long bench-like cars and enjoy the 6–MPH adventure that included a series of mild hills and valleys. At the opposite end of the brief course, once riders had disembarked, attendants would transfer the car over to a parallel track, where passengers then reboarded. The journey was repeated in the opposite direction, returning riders to their starting point. The *Switchback Railway* was an instant success and spurred other inventors to improve on Thompson's effort.

The next Coney marvel was developed by Charles Alcoke and dubbed the *Serpentine Railway*. This ride differed from Thompson's version in that Alcoke arranged the course into a continuous loop, thereby eliminating the need for any switching of vehicles or passengers to other tracks.

In 1885, Philip Hinkle opened Coney's third roller coaster. He further improved on the previous two by having passengers ride in seats which faced forward, instead of using the cumbersome park bench–like seating found on the other rides. Not only was this coaster more comfortable, it was somewhat larger and faster, too.

The appearance of these rides and the competition between their owners was but a preview of the "great coaster wars" about to begin. Spreading like wildfire, various forms of the roller coaster would soon appear at amusement parks all over America. Thompson's ride was even exported to Paris, where it opened indoors as the *Montagnes Russes* (despite its American heritage) in 1888.

The term "roller coaster" is thought to have originated in Haverhill, Massachusetts, in 1887 at an enclosed skating rink that featured a toboggan-like ride built above the rink. Riders boarded toboggan sleds which were raised, elevator style, to the top of the device. The sleds then were eased on to the track, which consisted of hundreds of rollers, and they took off, following the gently graded track down to the main floor—the track weaving back and forth figure-8 style as it descended. This *Roller Toboggan*, as it was named, was invented by Stephen E. Jackman and Byron B. Floyd, and they claimed to also be the first to use the term "roller coaster;" i.e., passengers coasted along on rollers. The *Roller Toboggan* became quite popular and a number of these rides sprung up around the country until several serious accidents quelled their popularity.

THOMPSON *SWITCH-BACK RAILWAY*, CLEVELAND, OHIO

La Marcus Thompson's *Switch-Back Railway* coaster of 1884 at New York's Coney Island was considered the first "true" roller coaster and spawned similar rides at other parks, such as that shown here at Euclid Beach in Cleveland, Ohio. Signs on the Euclid Beach ride claimed it to be 1,000 feet long. *Amusement Park Books Inc.*

La Marcus Adna Thompson

Born in Ohio in 1848, La Marcus Adna Thompson was an accomplished carpenter and competent businessman before he turned 40. He is often credited with being the inventor of the roller coaster. While this is not entirely accurate, Thompson was the first in the United States to actually build and operate a gravity-powered device specifically for entertainment. He was supposedly inspired by the much larger and more elaborate Mauch Chunk-Summit Hill Switch Back Railroad that had been built at Mauch Chunk, Pennsylvania. He envisioned a contraption that could offer similar thrills but take up a much smaller piece of real estate.

The result was the *Switch Back Railway*, which opened at the burgeoning resort area of New York's Coney Island in 1884. Though the patent for this device was not officially recognized until early 1885, the ride itself proved an instant success and made Thompson a wealthy man.

The meager ride was fairly simple, amounting to little more than a pleasant, low-impact tour along the sandy dunes. However, it became unbelievably popular and was the spark in the proverbial powder keg that would ignite a building craze that would boggle the imagination. Despite some slump periods, that roller coaster-building craze would continue for more than 100 years and is still going strong as this book went to press.

While other inventors improved on the *Switchback Railway* design, Thompson again surprised the world with another new coaster concept: the *Scenic Railway*. Opened in Atlantic City, New Jersey, in 1887, the first *Scenic Railway* was a combination dark ride and roller coaster. The attraction featured trains of exquisitely hand-carved vehicles (complete with on-board brakemen to control the speed). They traveled high above the beach on the outdoor sections, but the indoor portions were what really made the ride stand out above the typical coaster of that era. *Scenic Railway* passengers were treated to an elaborate collection of stunts, painted tableaus of historical scenes, and other special effects. The novel and abundant use of electric lights played a major role in bringing the enclosed areas of the ride to life, offering the paying public something new and exciting.

Like his *Switchback Railway*, Thompson's new ride was very successful—so much so, in fact, that he formed the L. A. Thompson Scenic Railway Company in 1888 and began installing his fantastic new rides at parks across the country. It seemed that each successive Thompson *Scenic Railway* installation was more complex and impressive than its predecessor. One of the most elaborate examples of this ride was the *Scenic Railway* that opened on a pier in Venice, California, in 1910. This massive project, with its artificial mountains, Egyptian temple replicas, and other exotic features, was one of the most prosperous contraptions of its kind in the world.

Thompson's popularity and recognition grew with each passing year as he went on to create numerous examples of his work in North America and abroad. When he died in 1919, the Thompson Company survived through the efforts of Frank Darling and continued building coasters, one of which remains in operation at Rye, New York. Because so many designers took inspiration and guidance from Thompson, this industry pioneer's legacy and influence are still very much alive and well.

ENTRANCE TO SCENIC RAILWAY, VENICE, CAL.

SCENIC RAILWAY AT VENICE, CALIFORNIA

Generally regarded as his finest *Scenic Railway* installation was the ride at Venice, California. It included an elaborate boarding station through which riders zipped on an upper level during the ride. *B. Derek Shaw collection*

Loop the Loop, Coney Island, N.Y.

Coney Island

Contemporary historians and park fans are justifiably fascinated by the amusement industry's striking origins, and roller-coaster history is closely intertwined with the evolution of the amusement park. Epicenter of amusement park development is one of the most famous entertainment areas in America: Coney Island. Rare photographs depicting Coney Island during its heyday are truly magnificent, and descriptions of imaginative, sometimes devious creations that arose there make one long for a time machine.

Coney Island was not an amusement park per se, but an area of Brooklyn devoted to resorts and entertainment. Coney was obviously a prime location for ambitious showmen; this sandy beach on the edge of

the Atlantic Ocean drew them to Brooklyn like moths to a flame. Practically anyone who had the courage to give it a go at Coney Island in the early days was successful. What it was about that narrow strip of land just south of Manhattan that fueled such creativity remains a mystery. It is almost as if the area had been imbued with some potent, mystical energy that inspired and gave birth to a host of parks and attractions that even today seem downright otherworldly.

In 1895, Paul Boynton opened at Coney what is often referred to as America's first amusement park, Sea Lion Park. It was supposedly the first pleasure park to be completely enclosed and charge admission for entry. Sea Lion was home to water rides, a coasterlike boat ride called the Shoot-the-Chutes, animal acts,

CONEY ISLAND

In the late nineteenth century the then-leisurely resort area of New York's Coney Island began to emerge as a leading amusement and entertainment center. By the early twentieth century, Coney was ablaze in new electric lighting and featured a looping roller coaster, the *Loop-the-Loop*, built in 1904 and shown in this night scene. The ride proved uncomfortable to riders and had low passenger capacity; the looping-coaster concept would thus lay dormant until the 1970s. *David P. Oroszi collection*

and an early wooden looping coaster called the *Flip Flap*. The park was a huge success and was obviously an inspiration to others.

George C. Tilyou was one of those who watched Sea Lion with a careful, calculating eye. He traveled extensively, visiting other parks, world's fairs, and expositions to gather ideas for his own dream park. In 1897, he put his plans into motion and opened world-famous Steeplechase Park. Its opening is widely considered the catalyst that initiated the virtual explosion of Coney's amusement district.

The park itself was named after a contraption called the *Steeplechase Ride*, which simulated the then-popular sport of horse racing. On parallel runs of steel track, mechanical horses seating two riders each traveled along an undulating course. It was a very popular coaster-like experience that would be duplicated several times at other parks. Steeplechase also boasted numerous other rides and attractions, including a large enclosure holding a fun house with plenty of stunts to keep the crowds entertained. Even though Steeplechase (as well as other Coney parks) suffered multiple, devastating fires, it was always rebuilt, bigger and better than before, and it lasted until the mid-1960s.

As the nineteenth century drew to a close,

Bird's-eye View of Luna Park, Coney Island, N. Y.

LUNA PARK

Another sensational amusement complex to rise at Coney Island was Luna Park, opened in 1903. As with any park of the era worth its salt, Luna featured roller coasters, at least two of which are partially visible in this scene from the 1920s. Other parks bearing the "Luna" name sprung up across America. *B. Derek Shaw collection*

STEEPLECHASE PARK

One of the greatest amusement parks ever at Coney Island was Steeplechase Park, opened in 1897. It was unusual in that many of its rides and attractions were housed within a huge multi-window building, allowing for year-round entertainment. Noted for its unique rides and novel amusement devices, Steeplechase served as a play place for New Yorkers until the 1960s. This 1940s-era postcard showed one of the park's unusual roller coasters, the *Flying Turns*. *Scott Rutherford collection*

STEEPLECHASE PARK, CONEY ISLAND, N. Y.

"pleasure parks" began appearing across North America in greater numbers. This flourishing form of outdoor entertainment had spread as far as the West Coast, where piers stretching out into the Pacific Ocean featured one or more coaster rides. However, the action was really beginning to heat up back at New York's Coney, where it had all begun.

Coney Island was being transformed into a pleasure resort unlike any other. In 1903, on the site of the former Sea Lion Park, an amazing confection opened called Luna Park—a wonderland of ornate architecture and attractions draped with a half million incandescent lights. The public was dazzled. Just one year later, Dreamland opened across the street and outdid Luna's spectacle with larger towers and twice the wattage. It has been said that, in those days, most European immigrants' first glimpse of the New World was not the Statue of Liberty, but the fiery brilliance of Coney Island's legendary amusement parks lighting up the night sky. For those hopeful soon-to-be Americans arriving in the New World after sunset, such a sight was surely a breathtaking and memorable greeting.

With the venues growing more abundant each season, Coney Island became a virtual testing ground for new amusement devices, especially roller coasters. The traditional wooden roller coaster continued to evolve and improve. The amazing success of L. A. Thompson's *Switch Back Railway* had only been the beginning. The *Switch Back Railway* was superceded by continuous circuit coasters, chief among them the "Figure 8" coaster and the "Scenic Railway" format. Figure-8 coasters

FIGURE-8 COASTER

The Figure-8 coaster, so called on account of its track layout (if viewed from directly above), became a wildly popular coaster format at the turn of the century, and hundreds of them were built throughout America. This one at Luna Casino Park in Mansfield, Ohio, was quite typical of the Figure-8 coaster format, with very gentle dips and a back-and-forth descent from the lift hill. All were side-friction coasters, relying on high track side boards to guide the coaster cars through the course. *George Siessel collection*

LEAP THE DIPS, LAKEMONT PARK, PENNSYLVANIA

Despite the abundance of Figure-8 coasters in North America, only one survives on the continent: the *Leap The Dips* at Lakemont Park near Altoona, Pennsylvania. It's birth date is disputed, with some accounts stating 1898 while others say 1902. Regardless, the century-or-so-old ride was refurbished and rechristened in 1999, ready to thrill riders into the new millennium! This view shows the ride operating in 1982 prior to its hiatus and eventual rebuild. *Otto P. Dobnick*

VARIATIONS ON A THEME
Coaster Mutants

There were a number of unique rides and attractions designed and built during the early years of the amusement industry. Some of these worked quite well, while others did not. A few of the more outrageous contraptions dreamed up by imaginative inventors bordered on the bizarre and fortunately (or maybe unfortunately) never made it off the drawing boards.

Herein is a selection of roller coaster-related rides that made an impact on the industry and whose reverberations can still be felt today. It's apparent that some of these rides directly influenced modern designers, as updated versions of several of these classics may be enjoyed today.

Steeplechase Ride

The *Steeplechase* was a remarkable device directly inspired by the sport of horse racing which was popular on Coney Island in the late nineteenth century. Commissioned by George C. Tilyou for his own Steeplechase Park in 1897, this rather unconventional coaster proved to be an odd but lucrative venture. And in a sense, it is one of the very first steel roller coasters ever built.

The prototype version of the ride featured parallel rows of narrow steel track on which a series of wooden horses carrying two riders each "raced" up, down, and around Tilyou's 15-acre Steeplechase complex. The *Steeplechase* ride worked on the same principal as the roller coaster: a chain lift carried the horses to the highest point and gravity did the rest. The combined weight of the passengers determined the winner of each race. The spirit of competition made re-rides a common and profitable occurrence. There was probably even some betting.

Several modified examples of the ride were put into operation at

THE WHIRL-FLY

There was (and is) no shortage of creativity when it came to variations on the roller coaster theme. This postcard depicts a combination coaster and Ferris wheel. It was set to debut at Coney Island, of course, the testing ground for numerous rides over the years. Whether the Whirl-Fly was actually built is unknown. *B. Derek Shaw collection*

other parks around the country, including Kennywood near Pittsburgh and Forest Park in Chicago.

Though the original Coney Island installation was destroyed by a 1907 fire, it was rebuilt (with metal horses in place of the wooden ones) and operated successfully until Steeplechase Park closed in the mid 1960s. On a positive note, the Coney Island ride was saved and rebuilt in 1967 at Pirate's World in Dania, Florida. Known there as the *Grand National Steeplechase*, it operated in a reconfigured, more compact form through the mid 1970s and was mildly popular with the meager crowds.

After Pirate's World closed, legend has it that the ride was again dismantled, shipped north, and put into storage "somewhere" in the metropolitan New York area. It would be interesting indeed if some

SOAP BOX DERBY RACERS

On the opposite coast from Coney Island, Knott's Berry Farm in Southern California featured an unusual coaster based on the old *Steeplechase* horse-racing coaster device. The *Soap Box Derby Racers* placed riders in individual coaster cars made up to look like a kid's homemade soap-box race car. The cars, all straddling a single-rail track, "raced" each other through an undulating 4-lane course via gravity. This interesting holdover from the Steeplechase era was dismantled in the 1990s. *Otto P. Dobnick*

enterprising operator found this classic example of amusement industry history and returned it to pristine operating condition.

Interestingly, Arrow Development produced two brand new updated versions of the *Steeplechase* ride in the mid 1970s. The first of this pair was built at California's Knott's Berry Farm. It opened in 1976 with motorcycles in place of horses. In 1980, the motorcycles were replaced with low-slung, bobsled-like vehicles and the ride's name was changed to the *Soap Box Derby Racers*. This version was a bit longer than the original Coney Island ride and featured an interesting multi-layered layout. Unfortunately, Knott's Berry Farm recently replaced this wonderful retro-classic ride with a small Japanese looping coaster.

Arrow's other *Steeplechase* fared much better and is still in operation today. Located at Blackpool Pleasure Beach in northern England, this ride more closely resembles the original. Riders board horses in pairs and race around a long, convoluted, grassy obstacle course, leaping over fences and gliding around gently banked turns. Like Tilyou's original *Steeplechase* must have been for our ancestors, Blackpool's version is a pure joy to ride. Applause must go to Blackpool's Thompson family for having the foresight to keep this wonderful, historically important ride in operation.

Virginia Reels and Ticklers

These curious rides appeared at several parks around the world and are grouped among those that fall into the unusual-

VIRGINIA REEL

The lift hill of the *Virginia Reel* that once stood at Revere Beach near Boston, Massachusetts. *B. Derek Shaw collection*

but-surprisingly-popular category. Both consisted of running surfaces built upon inclined planes. Circular vehicles were raised to the highest point via chain lift and released to take their courageous human cargo on a relatively low-speed, but highly entertaining journey to the bottom.

*Virginia Reel*s utilized a side friction-like track that zig-zagged its way down to a couple of brisk, often tunneled helixes. Some of these *Reel*s were heavily themed like the *Scenic Railway*s of that era. The *Tickler*s, on the other hand, resembled something akin to a human pinball machine.

They were especially rambunctious rides. Upon release from the lift, the tublike cars began a haphazard descent, bouncing and spinning wildly as they plowed into curved sections of fencing and posts placed at strategic locations along the sloping platform. Obviously—and just as in a real pinball game—no two rides were the same, as pile-ups caused by the railings and other vehicles made for a very unpredictable and turbulent experience. Both rides were popular with the crowds who didn't mind being buffeted about.

All of the North American versions of these attractions were long ago dismantled, but a single, small variation of the ride remains in operation in Great Yarmouth on England's eastern coast. The last full-size *Virginia Reel* was located at Blackpool Pleasure Beach until 1982.

were side-friction rides (see Glossary) whose track layout was arranged in figure-8 fashion (as with the *Roller Toboggan*), with the track descending gently in tiers. By the turn of the century, every park worth its name had a Figure-8 coaster. *Scenic Railways* usually employed traditional railway-type flanged wheels riding on iron rails. Track layout varied wildly, though the dips were relatively gentle since the coaster cars were not locked to the track in any way. The trackage was often surrounded by manmade "scenery" depicting mountains and such, and tunnels were *de rigeur*.

Designers and inventors had become highly intrigued by the prospect of taking Thompson's original switchback concept and adding their own ideas. This intense focus resulted in extensive improvements in roller coaster technology, which in turn rapidly propelled the industry to amazing new heights. In some cases, the more radical inventors gave their rides something of a devilish twist. One such attraction was called *Drop-the-Dip*. Located at Coney Island, this side-friction ride was built in 1907 by Christopher Feucht and is often considered the first "high-speed" roller coaster—that is, a coaster with steep, deep drops that sent coaster cars or trains plunging and hurtling around curves. *Drop-the-Dip* was quite popular due to its untamed nature, but it burned to the ground not long after opening. Undaunted, Feucht rebuilt the ride with an added dash of wickedness. Its new name—*Rough Rider*—foretold that it was a comparatively violent ride for its time, and therefore it became an incredibly profitable venture.

SCENIC RAILWAY, VENICE, CALIFORNIA

The so-called *Scenic Railway* was another enormously popular coaster format that came in various forms. Unlike the standardized Figure-8 coaster, each *Scenic Railway* was often an individual work of art. Many featured elaborate theming, such as L. A. Thompson's installation at Venice Pier, near Los Angeles. *B. Derek Shaw collection*

SCENIC RAILWAY, CEDAR POINT, SANDUSKY, OHIO

The *Scenic Railway* at Ohio's popular Cedar Point amusement park featured real scenery as cars whisked along high structure among the tree tops. This postcard is dated August 5, 1912, and the sender had written on the back, "I wish you and John were here to take a ride with us for I would like to hear you laugh." And that's what it was all about. *David P. Oroszi collection*

The Ingersoll Influence

Frederick Ingersoll and his family are commonly regarded as the greatest early perpetuators of the American amusement park. Even though Coney Island was a major influence in the development of

stupendous examples of the amusement park concept, and the virtual birthplace of the American roller coaster, it was Ingersoll who initiated the expansion of the bustling pleasure park business across North America and eventually around the world.

Ingersoll took inspiration from Coney Island's Luna Park and began spreading the gospel of fun across the land. The first example was Pittsburgh's Luna Park, which opened in 1905. Like its namesake, it was extravagant beyond description, full of sensual design details and, of course, electric lights that complemented the many rides and attractions. Cleveland's Luna Park opened that same year and was equally impressive.

Ingersoll had a surefire recipe for success, and he duplicated the concept frequently. In the same vein, other formula parks—many bearing the name "White City" or "Electric Park"—mushroomed. Much like today's theme parks, these early traditional parks followed a proven plan and were phenomenally successful.

Ingersoll and his clan were also instrumental in the evolution of roller coasters. They began with side-friction rides (their first was a large racer at Pittsburgh's Kennywood in 1902), filling the Luna Parks in North America and abroad with exciting thrillers, the likes of which guests had never dreamed of. They eventually progressed to larger and more modern rides, all the

CHASE THROUGH THE CLOUDS

The *Chase Through the Clouds* roller coaster at Pennsylvania's Willow Grove Park, near Philadelphia, illustrated how massive coasters had grown by the 1920s, although they often still featured only mild dips. The next step in coaster evolution was to combine lofty support structure with steep drops. *Scott Rutherford collection*

while providing something of an amusement park boot camp for park men who would eventually rise through the ranks and become recognized names in the industry. Talented individuals like John Miller and Joe McKee were among the many coaster designers and builders who had early associations with the Ingersoll family. Today, those outside of the industry may not recognize his name, but Ingersoll's legacy and influence are very much alive.

The Wave Builds

The widespread availability of electric power by the turn of the century revolutionized America in many ways and even figured into the development of amusement parks and roller coasters. In larger cities, electric trolleys replaced horsecars and suddenly the trolley and its city-to-city cousin, the electric interurban, became the preferred system of local travel. Trolley or streetcar ("light rail" in today's parlance) systems fostered city growth and became key to efficiently transporting people to and from work in the city center. Transit companies extended their rail lines to accommodate the growth. Often the end of a particular line was a good distance from the city, and transportation companies needed an incentive to bolster ridership, especially on weekends and during

THE THRILLER
Seaside, Rockaway Beach, L.I.

summer holidays when ridership was slack. The solution? Build an amusement park at the end of a route.

Commonly referred to as "trolley parks" and often owned and operated by the transit company, these facilities proved quite popular. They offered convenient day trips away from the crowded inner cities, and during summer weekends and evenings it became a familiar practice for families to make an event out of a visit to these trolley parks. They would pack picnic lunches and board the trolleys in the morning for a breezy journey out to an amusement park, often located in an attractive rural, relatively undeveloped area. Upon arrival at the park's station, guests would disembark to spend the entire day swimming, boating, playing games of chance, and enjoying rides—including the most alluring new thrill of them all, the roller coaster.

The brilliant concept of the trolley park quickly spread all across the country. Though numerous transit companies eventually were driven out of business by the automobile in the 1920s or the Depression that

followed, the trolley parks themselves often survived. Most notable among them is Pittsburgh's Kennywood Park. (In an interesting twist, the modern Great America theme park at Santa Clara, California, today is served by a new trolley line.)

Many amusement parks were constructed on the banks of rivers and sizable lakes, making them accessible not only by transit lines but also via fleets of elaborate steamships and paddle wheelers. Cincinnati's Coney Island, Louisville's Fontaine Ferry Park, and Crystal Beach in southern Ontario near Buffalo, New York, were all excellent examples of amusement parks that thrived off patrons arriving on various forms of water transportation.

Even though there were amusement parks in virtually every major city around the country during the turn-of-the-century era, the U.S. population base was still concentrated on the East Coast. Naturally, that's where much of the action was centered. Though New York's Coney Island was the nucleus of the amusement nebula, numerous parks and wooden roller

coasters were built near the sea or even atop it on piers over the waves. From New England to the Florida coast, seaside amusement parks were alive with the sounds of surf, laughter, music, and the memorable sounds of roller coasters—the clanking of the chain lift, the roar of the train down the first drop, and the screams of delighted (and terrified) riders.

By 1919 there were an estimated 1,500 roller coasters in operation in North America alone. In just over a decade, literally hundreds of new amusement parks and roller coasters were built. From New York to Los Angeles, Miami to Seattle, and in nearly every sizable city in the U.S. and Canada there existed amusement parks. With the rise in popularity of the automobile during the Roaring Twenties and the general upswing in the economy, people tended to move farther outside of city centers. The automobile's proliferation made traveling a greater distance for recreation convenient, affordable, and attractive. Consequently, competition increased between older urban parks and their new counterparts being erected past the city limits. To be truly competitive and profitable, parks scrambled to build the latest and greatest roller coasters they could.

The golden age of roller coasters was about to go into high speed.

COASTER CONSTRUCTION AT RIVERVIEW PARK, CHICAGO

A large side-friction racing coaster is in the final stages of construction at Chicago's famed Riverview Park. This ride is just one in a long line of Riverview roller coasters. Note that there are at least three other wooden coasters visible in this early 1900s view: a *Scenic Railway* to the immediate left of the new coaster; another racer in the upper left; and a simple Figure-8 side-friction ride at upper right. *Chicago Historical Society; photo No. ICHi–29363*

SCENIC RAILWAY SURVIVOR

Originally built in 1920, this is one of the few *Scenic Railways* still in operation. Located at Dreamland in Margate, England, this exquisite wooden ride has operated for nearly a century in basically the same manner, and it provides a sharp constrast to the new steel looper in the distance. A simple cable lift system hoists the heavy trains up the dual lift hills while an on-board brakemen controls the speed during the ride's gentle dips and sweeping turns. This is a must-ride for anyone seriously interested in roller coaster history. *Scott Rutherford*

The Golden Years

The Roller Coaster Comes of Age: 1920–1940

CONEY ISLAND
CYCLONE

An unprecedented number of roller coasters were built during the post-World War I years, among them one that would reign as arguably the most famous in the world during the twentieth century—the *Cyclone* at Coney Island, Brooklyn, New York. Though hardly the largest in the land, it remains as the coaster by which all others are judged. This colorized view shows the ride in the 1930s. *David P. Oroszi collection*

With the reservoir of roller coaster technology increasing steadily as the new century unfurled, the amusement industry was unconsciously being primed for the creative explosion that would soon begin—an era we know now as the first "golden age" of the roller coaster. Just exactly when this new era began is subject to debate, but coaster historians often point to 1912—the year that coaster engineer John Miller patented the "Miller Under Friction Wheel." Also known as the "upstop wheel," this arrangement—which virtually locked coaster cars to the tracks—had far-reaching implications.

Now, coasters could feature extremely steep drops, sharp horizontal and vertical curves and relentless speed—all of which the public was clamoring for as they grew nonchalant about figure-8 and scenic-railway-type coasters. (Of course, the upstop wheel by necessity led to another Miller patent, that for a locking safety bar on coaster cars. The fact that coaster cars equipped with under-friction wheels couldn't fly off the track didn't mean that passengers couldn't fly out of the train.) As the 1910s marched on—mostly toward war, unfortunately—the new technology began to take hold. Had it not been for World War I (1914–1918), the coaster's true golden age might have indeed begun earlier than the 1920s.

By the end of the conflict, a war-weary American public was eager to return to the good life. Fostered in part by postwar optimism and the self confidence that came with America's new role as a world leader, the U.S. economy by 1922 was experiencing a dramatic rebound. Simultaneously, a new generation infused with a refreshing spirit of frivolity was coming of age. Somewhat rebellious and daring, its members refused to conform to what they considered the stifling, old-fashioned mindset of their parents. A bold new attitude drove this iconoclastic segment of the populace to seek more adventurous distractions of the recreational variety. Fueled by the boom in private auto ownership, amusement parks enjoyed new growth. And their roller coasters provided the very escapism the public craved.

The Roaring Twenties

The "Roaring Twenties" was a raucous era that could not have been more aptly named, especially when speaking in terms of amusement parks and

V-23. AMUSEMENTS ON THE PIER, VENICE, CALIFORNIA.

VENICE PIER, CALIFORNIA

Early in the twentieth century, coasters quickly became major drawing cards for amusement areas. Coasters are prominent in this 1920s-era view of the ocean front at Venice, near Los Angeles. Pictured beside the Noah's Ark walk-through attraction is the prototype *Bobs* coaster built by Prior & Church in 1921 (note the unusual covered lift and first drop). The larger wooden coaster is the *Big Dipper*, an early John Miller ride which was, ironically, owned and operated by Prior & Church. *Scott Rutherford collection*

SIDE FRICTION IN TWILIGHT

By World War I, the side-friction coaster had pretty much reached its maximum potential in terms of wildness, as illustrated by this scene of a large side-friction ride, the *Jack Rabbit* at Revere Beach, Massachusetts. Faster coasters with more convoluted trackage or "negative G" hills would require under-friction wheels and their more-simplified track construction. *B. Derek Shaw collection*

On the Jack Rabbit, Revere Beach, Mass.

roller coasters. During this frenetic era, the wooden coaster underwent a dramatic and relatively rapid transformation from novelty amusement device to the true king of the midway. Ever larger and more spectacular roller coasters brought in the crowds.

Each amusement park was in fact a business, and the owners knew that grand attractions were required to make their operation the public's venue of choice. Many of the early side-friction coasters and *Scenic Railways* were becoming passé, and parks found themselves competing not only with each other, but with other evolving forms of entertainment. Radio was no longer a novelty, sound had been added to motion pictures, and dancing to big bands had become quite popular.

The public itself had changed, too. It seemed as if people had developed an insatiable appetite for excessively thrilling rides and attractions. The 1920s had become a magical time of unbridled optimism, and the sense of fearlessness pervading the country was intoxicating. Wisely recognizing the public's new disposition, park owners initiated a whirlwind of

WAVING FROM THE *WILDCAT*

A trainload of flappers and their gentlemen ham it up on the new wild and woolly *Wildcat* coaster at Woodside Park in Philadelphia circa 1927. *PTC.*

WILDCAT, OPEN FOR BUSINESS

Philadelphia Toboggan Company built the Woodside *Wildcat* during the winter of 1926–27. The ride included a tunneled approach to the lift hill (a train has just exited the tunnel in this view, probably taken shortly after the ride's opening in 1927), swooping drops, and a tunneled conclusion. PTC—now known as Philadelphia Toboggan Coasters—still manufactures coaster trains. Construction techniques for wood coaster trains remain relatively unchanged (most technology advancements have involved the safety-bar locking system), and today's PTC trains are strikingly similar to those in these two views. *PTC*

that mercilessly tossed riders about as seemingly out-of-control trains flew through their circuits—thanks to John Miller's under-friction wheel. Few people complained. After all, this was a time of barely restrained madness, and the public willingly embraced the reckless atmosphere it found in its amusement parks, especially on the often-ferocious roller coasters. For thrillseekers and adventurers, it was the best of times.

The Minds and Companies Behind the Mania

Of course, this explosion in roller coaster creativity did not occur by chance. Talented and resourceful individuals made it all possible, and a quick perusal of industry history reveals a core group of names and manufacturers behind the wave of wooden-coaster installations that occurred during the first golden age of roller coasters.

The most prolific designers imprinted their distinctive styles—like unique three-dimensional signatures rendered in wood and steel—onto each of their rides as clearly as a fingerprint. These personal architectural aspects are clearly evident in old photographs, postcards, and even the few golden-age coasters that survive today.

And to add to their credit, these designers worked their magic without extensive training or the luxury of computers and calculators. Through painstaking experimentation, these pioneers learned by their own trial and error as well as from each other and used an innate sense of how structure and dynamics behaved to create some of the most amazing thrill machines humankind then had ever seen. These industry pioneers envisioned, designed, and then erected rides that could almost be considered monuments. The work of these craftsmen thrilled millions, but rarely did any receive any recognition outside of the amusement industry. In some cases their names went unnoticed until the coaster renaissance—and a new, unprecedented awareness of coaster history—that would close out the twentieth century.

Not only did individuals play key roles in the golden age of roller coasters, but so did several companies. Firms like the Philadelphia Toboggan Company, National Amusement Device, T. M. Harton

OLD AND NEW, SIDE BY SIDE
A view down the first drop of the new *Thriller* coaster built by Philadelphia Toboggan Company in 1924 at Cleveland's Euclid Beach. The coaster stood next to the *Derby Racer* (later known as the *Racing Coaster*) whose double-track course is immediately to the right. The *Thriller*'s second hill—plainly visible between the photographer's position and the *Thriller*'s first turn in the distance—was lowered shortly after the ride opened to increase pace and introduce a "negative G" effect at the apex of the newly profiled hump. *PTC*

roller-coaster construction. Ride designers and builders were hired to create the most thrilling rides then technically feasible. This incessant demand for larger and more complex coasters brought out the best and brightest engineers and dreamers, and it was almost as if these designers had somehow anticipated the need for something more. They were ready to give the thrillseekers exactly what they wanted—and then some.

The new breed of wooden roller coaster was approaching the 100-foot-high mark. Drops had become steeper, turns tighter, and track layouts unpredictable to riders. Some designers built coasters

Company, and the Ingersoll Company, along with coaster-building families such as the Vettels and Pearces were all erecting coasters as quickly as technically possible. (Considering the amount of wood being fashioned into thrill machines, it was probably a glorious period to be in the timber business as well.) Some of the key individuals and firms of the golden age follow.

John A. Miller and Harry Baker

John A. Miller has already been mentioned for what is perhaps one of the single most important contributions to roller-coaster evolution: the under-friction wheel. But his impact on roller-coaster evolution and design went well beyond that. Known by some as "The Master," Miller was the most prolific and influential designer and builder active during the coaster's first golden age.

Known today as the father of the high-speed roller coaster, Illinois-born (in 1872) Miller had been involved with coaster construction since before the turn of the century, at one time working for none other than La Marcus A. Thompson, builder of the first true American roller coaster (chapter 1). After

Racing Coasters

As the wooden roller coaster's popularity steadily increased as the twentieth century got under way, developers looked for ways to increase their profit margin as well as handle the growing crowds. The racing roller coaster was the perfect solution.

The idea was immediately embraced as park owners saw great potential offered by the racing concept. Not only did the racing coaster's multiple trains accommodate twice the number of patrons, the spirit of competition was readily apparent among riders. Returns were impressive. Further, because the parallel coaster tracks usually shared common structurework, racing coasters were economical to construct. Parks in effect got two coasters for the price of building one and a half.

James A. Griffiths, a talented designer of Scenic Railways who became L. A. Thompson's chief rival, is often credited for introducing the first modern racing coaster, in 1895. PTC, John Miller, Frederick Ingersoll, Joe McKee, Prior & Church, Andy Brown, the Vettels and practically every other talented designer also took a shot at the racing coaster. Many examples were produced during the early years of the twentieth century, and by the time Miller's upstop wheels came into play, the idea's full possibility was realized.

The years leading up to and encompassing the golden age saw many racing coasters constructed. Some of the most popular of the lot included the *Racer* at Kennywood Park near Pittsburgh; the *Racing Whippets* of West View Park also near Pittsburgh; the *Racing Coaster* at Euclid Beach, Cleveland; and the John Miller-designed triple racers at Louisville's Fontaine Ferry and State Fair Park near Dallas, Texas.

There are two basic types of racing coasters, continuous track and double track. By far the most common today are double-track racers which in essence are two parallel but independent track courses that happen to share the same supporting structure and usually the same profile. Both tracks can be operated or only one can be run if crowds are minimal; dispatching the trains so that they race (when both tracks are operated) is at the discretion of the ride operators.

Continuous-track racers have but a single track that doubles back on itself to create two parallel tracks. Outwardly, the coaster appears to have two separate but parallel tracks, including two lift hills, but riders boarding a train on the right platform of the station will return on the left platform, and vice versa. Each train makes two trips (unloading and loading riders between trips, as with any racing coaster) before it repeats any trackage. Because of the continuous track nature, both trains have to be released from the station more or less concurrently, or one eventually could catch up to the other.

Several racing coasters have appeared on the scene in recent years, but only three examples of the intriguing continuous-track concept remain: Kennywood's venerable John Miller-designed *Racer*; Charlie Paige's *Grand National* at England's Blackpool Pleasure Beach, and the Eddie Leis–designed *La Montaña Rusa at La Feria* in Mexico City.

Operated as intended, with trains truly racing, this breed of coaster brings a new dimension into the ride experience.

KENNYWOOD *RACER*

Several years ago, management at Pittsburgh's incomparable Kennywood Park mulled replacing its *Racer* with a newer attraction, but wisely reconsidered. Now over 70 years old and sporting newer trains and a station that in 1990 was restored to its 1927 grandeur, the *Racer* remains a favorite of park patrons and coaster enthusiasts. In this 1980 scene, members of the American Coaster Enthusiasts enjoy a spin on the *Racer* and its then-vintage trains. *Mike Schafer*

Coney Island, Cincinnati, Ohio

CINCINNATI'S CONEY ISLAND

Coney Island stood along the banks of the Ohio River (a situation which would lead to the park's downfall) near Cincinnati. In this aerial postcard view, the park's *Wild Cat* coaster is in the foreground (PTC, 1926) and the *Clipper* (PTC, 1937) is at far left. (The coaster-like ride adjacent to the *Wild Cat* is actually a mill chute water ride.) The *Clipper* featured a covered helix, which in this colorized scene has a red roof and is near ground level. *Randy Rasmussen collection*

CONEY'S COVERED COASTER

Coney Island also had a coaster called the *Twister* whose entire trackage was shrouded like a long covered bridge. Built by PTC in 1926 along with the *Wild Cat*, the *Twister* stood next to the lift hill of the *Sky Rocket*, a 1921 Miller & Baker coaster which is partially visible at right in the photo. The *Sky Rocket* was replaced by the *Clipper* in 1937, and the *Clipper* itself was replaced by the *Shooting Star* in 1947 with the latter utilizing the *Clipper*'s station, lift hill, and helix finale. Apparently, covered coasters never caught on—only a handful were built—and the *Twister* was soon dismantled. *PTC*

gaining a great deal of experience as an apprentice, he eventually opened his own engineering company based in what is now the south suburbs of Chicago at Homewood, Illinois.

He was a gifted man with an analytical mind who devised and patented over 100 roller coaster-related ideas early in his career. Interestingly, Miller's designs and concepts have changed little over the years. Though they have been updated to meet modern safety standards, many are still employed in one form or another on most of today's coasters. In addition to operating his own company, the prolific Miller lent his knowledge and expertise to many coaster-building firms at one time or another. Whether he acted as the ride's actual designer or as a consultant, Miller influenced an enormous number of the roller coaster projects of this era.

In 1920, Miller teamed up with contractor Harry Baker, and until they split in 1923, Miller & Baker, Inc.—with offices in New York's Grand Central Terminal as well as Los Angeles and Chicago (Homewood)—managed to build vastly popular coasters all over North America, a few of which still exist. (They also dealt with non-coaster amusement devices.) Among the hallmarks of a John Miller-inspired coaster

were parabolic "camelback" hills, multiple straight or slightly angled drops that went all the way to the ground, and large, flat turns. His rides were enormously popular, and he was a trusted name in the industry, a designer to whom park owners turned again and again. Many of Miller's most profitable rides were racing coasters, in which trains "raced" on side-by-side tracks.

Some of Miller's most famous rides still in operation include the *Jack Rabbit*, *Racer*, and a portion of the

COASTER, DES MOINES, IOWA

John Miller was among the most prolific coaster designers of the golden era, and his work could (and can) be found from coast to coast. Shown in 1978 not long before it was dismantled, the *Coaster* at Riverview Park in Des Moines, Iowa, dated from the early 1920s and was a product of Miller & Baker, Inc. The train in this scene is from National Amusement Device and probably dates from the 1950s or early 1960s. Riverview closed shortly after nearby Adventureland theme park opened its first wood coaster, the *Tornado*, in 1978. *Mike Schafer*

LUCY'S COASTER

Celeron Park near Jamestown, New York, was a second home to comedienne Lucille Ball. She loved the park, spent much time there during the 1910s and 1920s, and for a time even worked there as a barker. Undoubtedly the assertive actress-in-the-making put in some serious riding time on the park's coasters, the best of which was the *Greyhound*, a classic which featured John Miller's hallmark "camelback" hills that went all the way to the ground. *B. Derek Shaw collection*

66. THE GREYHOUND, CELORON PARK, JAMESTOWN, N. Y.

Thunderbolt at Pittsburgh's Kennywood Park; *Roller Coaster* at Lagoon Park, Farmington, Utah; the *Big Dipper* at Geauga Lake, Aurora, Ohio; portions of the *Wild One* at Adventure World near Washington, D.C.; and a handful other others including the dormant *Thunderbolt* at New York's Coney Island, which sits in forlorn silence beside the sea, awaiting destruction.

Although John Miller reportedly spoke out against up-and-coming designers who built more radical coasters featuring heavily banked turns, super-elevated spiral drops, and other severe attributes (made possible, ironically, by Miller's own inventions), he knew he had to remain competitive. His response to the other designers' extreme coasters were several rides that were terrifying in their own right, perhaps the most famous being the legendary *Cyclone* (1928–1958) at Puritas Springs park near Cleveland, Ohio. This vicious ride joins a select few of the golden-age classics that are counted among the most severe rides ever built during that period. Though Miller preferred to build traditional coasters, he proved he could indeed compete with the more adventurous designers of the era.

After he split from Miller, Baker continued in the business and even competed in the extreme-coaster wars with his own *Whippet* designs. Though little documentation has come to light about these intense rides, they live on in coaster lore as truly wanton thrillers.

Although Harry Baker's post-Miller & Baker efforts are largely overshadowed by John Miller's accomplishments, Baker was one of the major players responsible for the Coney Island *Cyclone*, a ride that is often considered to be the most famous roller coaster in the world. Working with Vernon Keenan's design, Baker and his team built and opened the *Cyclone* in 1927. Obviously, Baker was well versed in quality construction: In the 1980s the *Cyclone* was declared a National Historic Landmark and is still

SCREECHING EAGLE, AMERICANA PARK

Not far from Kings Island theme park near Cincinnati, Ohio, sat a traditional park featuring a classic, textbook example of a John Miller coaster. Relocated to Americana Park near Le Sourdesville in the 1930s, the 1927-built *Screeching Eagle* provided riders a walloping ride with stomach-floating plunges until the park closed at the end of the 1999 season. *Mike Schafer*

CONEY ISLAND *CYCLONE*

Though compact by today's standards, the *Cyclone* in Brooklyn, New York, remains the king of coasters—the standard bearer by which all others are measured. Trans-Atlantic aviator Charles Lindbergh is said to have claimed the *Cyclone* was more exciting than barnstorming in a plane. A 1927 product from the peak of the golden age of roller coasters, the *Cyclone*—shown in 1980—remains among the Top Ten best coasters ever to rule the earth. *Mike Schafer*

CYCLONE ENTRANCE

Patrons line up on a blistering summer day in 1985 to purchase tickets for the *Cyclone*. At that time, a single ride cost $2; rerides (without detraining) were a dollar. Although part of Astroland Amusement Park, the *Cylone* actually stands by itself within a fenced-in lot at the corner of Surf and 10th in Brooklyn's Coney Island district. *Otto P. Dobnick*

thrilling riders today. The success of Keenan and Baker's *Cyclone* led the two men to collaborate on another coaster, in Poughkeepsie, New York.

Fred Church and Thomas Prior

Comprised of a supremely talented and trailblazing engineer named Fred Church and his business partner Thomas Prior, Prior & Church was ready to show the world what it had been doing at the coastal amusement districts near Los Angeles. Much like New York's Coney Island, the Venice, Ocean Park, and Santa Monica areas had long been West Coast testing grounds for new amusement devices. Several designers—among them L. A. Thompson and John Miller—had come here to install their own coasters. They had all been successful ventures, and some of these designers had even worked on projects with Church and Prior.

Initially, Church and Prior had worked with John Miller as well as Joe McKee and Charlie Paige during the design and construction of Frederick Ingersoll's *Race Thru the Clouds* in Venice. This enormous side-friction racing coaster was the largest of its kind when it opened in 1911. Sometime after that successful project, Church and Prior decided to strike out on their own. They formed the Venice Amusement Company and continued to build and operate amusement devices in the Venice area until Thomas died in 1918. His son, Frank Prior, joined Church, and together they went on to develop a line of roller coasters unlike anything the world had ever seen.

While the majority of Miller's rides consisted of tall camelback hills and relatively simple layouts, Fred Church eventually became far more daring in the execution of his designs. In 1921, Church opened the first of what became known as his "Bobs"-type coasters on one of the ocean piers at Venice. Drawing on his mechanical engineering skills and previous experience in the amusement field, Church devised a

new type of train flexible enough to negotiate the twisted creations of which he was dreaming. The unique nine-car *Bobs* trains consisted of narrow, flanged-wheeled, two-passenger (but single-seat), toboggan-like cars in which passengers were seated one in front of the other rather than side-by-side. A unique three-point suspension system gave this rolling stock its magic. The train was led by a four-wheeled pilot car with a divided body and pivoting nosepiece, and each succeeding single-axle car was connected by ball-and-hitch joint. This arrangement caused the wheels of each car to bear equally upon the track at all times, ensuring a smooth, very controlled, serpentinelike ride.

Within the next two years, Church sold several more of his small *Bobs* coasters, but in 1923 his expertise and genius knocked the industry out of complacency. His introduction of the high-banked turn made others in the field stand up and take notice of his work. The coaster that first showcased Fred Church's true brilliance was the *Giant Dipper* that opened on Pickering Amusement Pier in Ocean Park,

BLUE STREAK, WOODSIDE PLEASURE PARK, POUGHKEEPSIE

The Coney Island *Cyclone* was not a one-hit wonder of the Vernon Keenan/Harry Baker duo. The same year that the *Cyclone* opened (1927), Keenan and Baker also built the *Blue Streak* at Woodside Pleasure Park near Poughkeepsie, New York. At either 127 or 140 feet—depending on what source is to be believed—the *Blue Streak* held title to being the highest coaster in North America. The two deepest drops were not at the start of the ride, but at the end, as this aerial view of the coaster shows (the lift hill is at the far end). The coaster's design took advantage of the terrain to accomplish this record—a title not topped until the *Beast* opened at Kings Island in 1979. Alas, the *Blue Streak* had long since disappeared by that time. *B. Derek Shaw collection*

404:—Cyclone at Night, Revere Beach, Mass.

24883

California. This ride was an enlarged *Bobs* coaster with severe banking, steep drops, and nonstop action. The larger and somewhat improved Church trains now featured more practical side-by-side seating. But the *Giant Dipper* was only the beginning of what Church had in mind.

In 1924, Fred Church opened his first coaster east of the Mississippi. Built by the Traver engineering Company (a firm that would play a major role in the extreme-ride competition within a few years) at Riverview Park in Chicago, the Riverview *Bobs* immediately outgrossed the parks other coasters three to one—and would continue to do so for the next 43 years. Some of Riverview's other coasters just happened to be Miller-designed rides, and this fact was not lost on the industry. The public was ready for more radical coasters, and it was Fred Church who in his own quiet, calculated manner was

REVERE BEACH *CYCLONE*

This night scene of the exemplary Revere Beach *Cyclone* clearly showcases thrilling hallmarks of master designer Fred Church. *B. Derek Shaw collection*

THE *DRAGON COASTER*

At Rye, New York, stands Playland Park and its coaster treasure. At this Art Deco wonderland on Long Island Sound in 1929, Fred Church opened his *Dragon Coaster*—truly a gem of the golden age. Though nowhere near as terrorizing as his *Bobs* rides, the *Dragon Coaster* nonetheless delivered a fast-paced ride (thanks in part to its flanged-wheel trains) through a complex maze of trackage that included a trip through the entrails of a "dragon." In this 1987 scene, the ride still sported its museum-quality Church-designed trains, which, because of parts availability, have since been replaced with modern fiberglass rolling stock. *Otto P. Dobnick*

the man responsible for the extreme coaster wars that lasted marked the later years of the golden age of roller coasters.

He built numerous *Bobs*-style coasters over the next several years. Though every ride shared traits of the ones that came before it, each was an individual work of art. These rides featured steep drops, swooping turns, stacked trackage, and unpredictable directional changes. And though they were intense, they were not terribly violent. Passengers were tossed around on the turns due to Church's practice of keeping a good deal of lateral forces intact, but the heavily padded trains were comfortable and absorbed the forces exerted on riders.

Church's trains themselves were a marvel to behold. Appearing like writhing serpents, they flawlessly negotiated his rides' convoluted layouts in a smooth, fluid manner. But the coasters' structures were even more visually absorbing and aesthetically pleasing. Fred Church above all else was an artist. Though his rides' wooden trestlework functioned basically as support for the twisted track, Church painstakingly arranged the timbers in a way that almost sang of elegance and grace, and it is apparent that he intentionally designed his rides to be picturesque as well as physically thrilling.

Though Church created an impressive number of Bobs-style coasters during his illustrious career, his masterpiece was the incomparable *Aeroplane Coaster* at Playland Park in Rye, New York. Other notable Church rides included the *Cyclone* at Revere Beach, Massachusetts; the *Bobs* at Bellevue Park (Manchester, England); and his only racing coaster, the magnificent *Cyclone Racer* at Long Beach, Calif.

Built by Traver Engineering in 1930 on a pier above the Pacific Ocean, the *Cyclone Racer* was an amazing accomplishment of pier and roller-coaster engineering. Sadly, it was destroyed in 1968 as the City of Long Beach sought to modernize and upgrade its image. As many Long Beach residents later realized, the result was the unforgivable destruction of an American classic that had safely thrilled literally millions of people over the years and appeared in more motion pictures than any other roller coaster.

continued on page 44

SPECIAL NOTES IN COASTER HISTORY
What's in a Name?

Roller coasters have had names for almost as long as there have been coasters. From the succinct (*Coaster*) to the outrageous (*Hurler*, as in "losing one's lunch"), a ride's name often speaks of its personality. And, like baby names, there seems to be trends as to what's "in."

Once past the *Scenic Railway* era, the earliest popular names often involved variations of the word "dip," as in *Big Dipper*, *Dip the Dips*, and *Leap The Dips*. "Pippin," which is a variety of apple, was another popular name in the 1910s and 1920s, although the connection between fruit and coasters is a bit puzzling.

Some parks didn't apply a specific name to their resident coaster (especially when they only had one) and instead just applied the generic label *Coaster* or *Roller Coaster*, as illustrated here by the sign on the station of the coaster at Joyland Park in Wichita, Kansas.

Many parks simply adopted

There's little doubt as to what kind of ride this is, at Joyland Park, Wichita, Kansas. *Scott Rutherford*

the manufacturers' product-line name for their new installations, and soon amusement centers were populated by *Bobs*'s, *Cyclones*, *Wildcats*, *Flying Turns*, and *Corkscrews*. As coaster awareness grew to a national scale, it became necessary to identify them by including the park's name, as in "Lakeside *Cyclone*" or "the Idora *Wildcat.*"

Celestial and weather phenomenons have enjoyed steady popularity as ride names: *Comet*, *Shooting Star*, *Tornado*, *Skyrocket*, *Twister*, *Thunderbolt*, *Jetstream*, and *Zephyr*. And above all, perhaps, animals have inspired coaster names from the early years to the present: *Jack Rabbit*, *Anaconda*, *Viper*, *Beast*, *Dragon*, *Wolverine Wildcat*, *Raging Wolf Bobs*, *Loch Ness Monster*, and various *Eagles*.

But unique and clever names do exist, and some favorites include the *Psyclone*, *Shivering Timbers*, *Mister Twister*, *Alpengeist* (translated: mountain ghost), and, of course, the *Hurler*.

WORLD'S GREATEST RIDE

The *Cyclone Racer* at the Pike in Long Beach, California was the only racing coaster that esteemed designer Fred Church ever created. Constructed in 1930 on a long pier stretching out into the Pacific, the *Cyclone Racer* was truly a magnificent sight to behold. Its twin lift hills climbed 110 feet above the beach (96 feet from pier level) and sent the racing trains into a fantastic collection of steep drops, swooping turns, and other surprises buried deep within the dense superstructure. With a track length of 3,400 per side, riders enjoyed a long, speedy tour of the complex course and the occasional splash of sea spray as trains negotiated the lower ocean-end turns. Due to its proximity to Hollywood, the *Cyclone Racer* was utilized in a host of feature films and television shows. Sadly, this noble ride was destroyed in 1968 during the City of Long Beach's attempt to improve its image. No racing coaster built since has approached the splendor of the *Cyclone Racer*. *David Johnson*

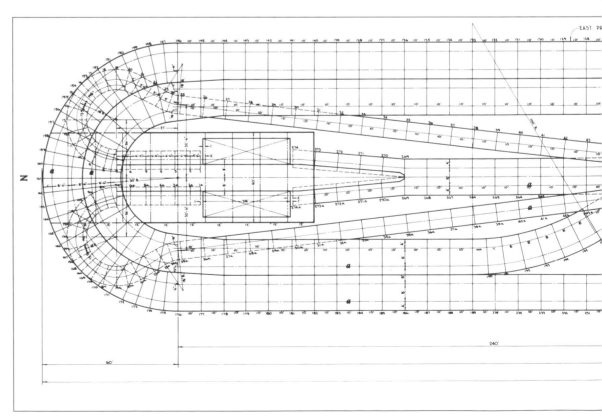

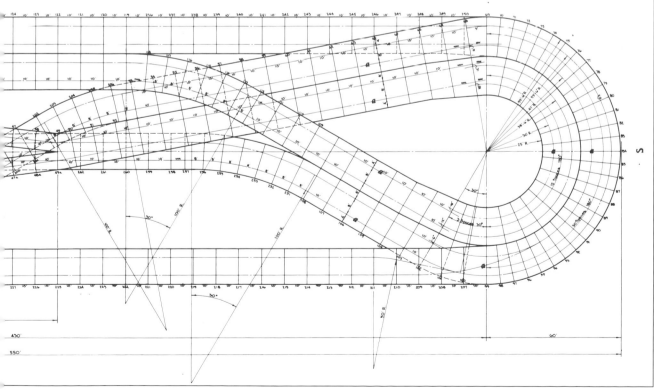

CYCLONE RACER ENGINEERING DRAWING

This top view engineering plan of the world-famous *Cyclone Racer* was drawn by Randy Rasmussen, a civil engineer in Eureka, California. An admitted Fred Church devotee, Rasmussen created this rendering from the actual blueprints used to build and maintain the legendary *Cyclone Racer*. The blueprints were found in the famous ride's station office just before it was leveled. *Randy Rasmussen*

continued from page 41

Though all the above-mentioned thrillers are long gone, we are fortunate indeed to have three Church-inspired rides still in operation today. These beautiful rides offer a revealing glimpse of this artist's true genius and passion for his work: the *Giant Dipper* at Santa Cruz (California) Beach and Boardwalk, a product of the Looff family of designers, but one using Church patents; the *Giant Dipper* at Belmont Park, San Diego; and the *Dragon Coaster* in Rye, New York.

Harry Traver

Born in 1877, Harry Traver forever will be known as a maverick in the amusement industry. Like most creative people, Traver was a dreamer. In amusement circles, he is often compared to Walt Disney because of his outlandish and unorthodox ideas and schemes. But also like Disney, some of Traver's "dreams" became historical legends.

CHURCH'S HAUNTED COASTER

Wedged on a narrow slice of property at New York's Coney Island was a Fred Church masterpiece that thrilled riders for more than half a century. Unveiled in 1926 as yet another *Bobs* in the series of coasters that made Fred Church famous, the Coney Island *Bobs* (later renamed *Tornado*) was built by the venerable L. A. Thompson Co. and featured an unbelievably convoluted, diabolical track arrangement, as this view from the late 1920s readily illustrates. For years there were reports that La Marcus Thompson could be seen working in the ride's ornate tower—never mind that he had died several years before his company built the ride. Overshadowed by its more-famous cousin, the *Cyclone*, just down the street, the *Tornado*'s loss in 1978 went relatively unnoticed—until interest in coasters from an historical standpoint fully blossomed at the onset of the 1980s. *Charles Jacques collection*

After amassing a small fortune with a popular ride he invented called the *Circle Swing* (a contraption that was supposedly inspired by Traver's observance of sea gulls idly circling a ship's mast at sea), he opened the Traver Engineering Company in Beaver Falls, Pennsylvania, in 1919. The well-known firm developed a number of classic rides, such as the *Laff in the Dark, Tumble Bug, Custer Cars, Merry Mix Up, Jazz Railway* (a small coaster that was something of a predecessor to the *Wild Mouse*), and a steel-structured, wood-track roller coaster.

Traver's company also acted as a sales rep and contractor for Prior & Church, building several of their *Bobs* coaster installations. Traver's credits with Church-designed coasters included the Long Beach *Cyclone Racer*, Riverview Park *Bobs*, and Revere Beach *Cyclone*. But it was Traver's three infamous Giant *Cyclone* Safety Coasters that earned him the notorious reputation as an extremist.

After working as a contractor to build several of Fred Church's *Bobs* coasters, Harry Traver and his team used the knowledge they had gained to modify the articulated Church-style coaster trains and used steel in place of wood for the coaster support structure. The resulting rides were marketed as "Giant *Cyclone* Safety Coasters." These fearsome steel-structured, wood-tracked monsters were built at New Jersey's Palisades Park (1927), Revere Beach near Boston (1927), and Crystal Beach in southern Ontario, Canada, near Buffalo, New York (1927). The Revere Beach model was named *Lightning* while the others employed the *Cyclone* name.

All three rides (along with a fourth, smaller but no less wicked example built the same year at Oregon's Oaks Park) featured nearly identical layouts, including a height of around 100 feet, devilishly banked drops, turns, and a ferocious ground-level figure-8 maneuver

continued on page 50

CRYSTAL BEACH *CYCLONE*

What was the most ferocious coaster ever built? The debate will never be settled, but one coaster consistently enters the discussion—Harry Traver's terrifying *Cyclone* at Crystal Beach, Ontario. The *Cyclone* and its near twins in New Jersey and Massachusetts featured a radical track arrangement that was truly hellish, with abrupt changes in track profile that threw riders about their seats and caused an excess of injuries. For today's coaster enthusiasts, such would be nirvana, but for the general public it meant few repeat riders, and shortly Traver's "Giant *Cyclone* Safety Coasters" vanished into history. *Charles Jacques collection*

Golden Age Classics

Hundreds of wooden roller coasters were built during the golden years, and each offered a distinctive, entertaining ride experience. Nonetheless, a select cadre of coasters erected during the first boom stood out above the rest. These rides reached a wider audience due to the originality instilled in them by their designers. In a few rare instances, some of these coasters were so popular (or fortunate) that they survived the industry's dark days and are now enjoying a resurgence in popularity. Here are a few of the more notable classic rides, including both vanished and surviving:

AIRPLANE COASTER—Playland Park, Rye, New York: This ride is considered Fred Church's ultimate. Into the *Aeroplane Dips*, as the ride was originally named, Church poured all previous experience he had accumulated with his earlier *Bobs* coasters, creating a thriller unlike any other. He had learned to manipulate the behavior of wooden roller coasters to a degree that other ride designers of his day had not even dreamed possible.

Debuting in 1928, the *Aeroplane Dips* was a multi-layered, compact twister that seemed to go on forever. It stood nearly 90 feet high, with a 3,000-plus-foot-long course comprised of a mysterious collection of swoop turns, spirals, and quick directional changes—mysterious because they were partially obscured by the ride's impressive structurework. One of the most memorable (and frightening to some) sections of the ride was the so-called "whirlpool." This steep spiral-to-the-ground maneuver simulated an airplane's tailspin dive. The whirlpool was situated right next to the loading platform for maximum effect, so that the roaring train, vibrating structure, and continuous screaming very probably gave park guests cause for alarm.

Because of its intense (though not violent) nature, the *Airplane*, as it was finally known, developed a reputation as a true white-knuckle experience that few approached casually. The

RYE PLAYLAND'S *AEROPLANE DIPS*

The new *Aeroplane Dips* coaster looms above the parking lot at Playland Park in Rye, New York, shortly after its 1928 opening. The right-side portion of the ride is the lift hill crest and banked turn leading to the first drop. *George Siessel collection*

notion that Playland's star attraction was outright dangerous was unfounded and merely a product of the overwhelming *perceived* danger that this coaster induced in riders and spectators alike. Church's heavily cushioned, articulated, 10-car single-seat trains safely negotiated the twisted layout effortlessly, maintaining an impressive rate of velocity despite the extreme acrobatics they performed.

Unfortunately, Playland and the *Airplane* were municipally owned. In 1957, Westchester County changed insurance providers, and the new, overly cautious firm decided that the ride required additional safety measures if it were to remain operational. That condemnation, along with a small contingent of local residents who considered the ride too much (and whom reportedly fostered a rumor of a death on the ride), spelled the end for the *Airplane Coaster*. It was destroyed that same year. According to those who have ridden it, its equal has never been built.

BOBS—Riverview Park, Chicago: Riverview had an impressive number of wooden roller coasters throughout its history, but none approached the popularity of the *Bobs*. Designed by Fred Church and built by Traver Engineering in 1924, it did not follow Church's typical compact *Bobs* layout. Because it was rather spread out, the vehicles were able to build up more speed than most twisters of that period. With three 11-car trains operating, the *Bobs* was a high-capacity machine that always provided a powerful adventure to riders who still talk about the ride in hushed, reverent tones.

From its 87-foot-high (some say 75 feet) lift hill, trains dropped into a vicious "fan turn" that slammed riders to one side and then swept them up and over the first drop toward the first of two tight "water wing" drop curves. The *Bobs'* relentless pace and unorthodox characteristics made it a hit in its first season.

Over the years, Riverview's *Bobs* received much hype through

RIVERVIEW *BOBS*

Despite its wild reputation, the *Bobs* at Chicago's Riverview Park, shown in May 1960, was a compact, low-profile coaster with a lift hill that was only 87 feet high. Nonetheless, it delivered a fantastic ride, full of banked turns and unpredictable twists through tiered trackage. The coaster made the *Guiness Book of Records*—not for height, speed, or recklessness, but for the number of lost earings that had been collected by the time the ride closed for good in 1967: over 7,000. *John McCarthy photo, Chicago Historical Society; photo No. ICHi–00037*

newspaper advertising and in radio spots broadcast all over the Midwest on WLS Radio, one of the most popular and powerful AM stations of the 1960s. Advertising claimed that *Bobs* trains shot along at 90 MPH, which was physically impossible given the ride's parameters (50 MPH was closer to the truth). But since the *Bobs* featured multi-tiered trackage, 50 MPH *seemed* like 90 MPH to those aboard its serpentine trains sweeping through the structurework past bents and under beams.

Other Riverview attractions came and went, but the *Bobs* remained the undisputed king. In its 44 years of operation, it was never upstaged. In fact, park closing time was determined ultimately by the length of the line waiting to board the *Bobs*. Sadly, Riverview's demise was announced unexpectedly after its regular Labor Day closing in 1967. When the *Bobs* was ripped apart to make room for a mall, the world lost another legend.

CYCLONE—Astroland Amusement Park; Coney Island, Brooklyn, New York: Considered the most famous roller coaster on the planet, the venerable *Cyclone* seems to have led a charmed life. Even though it opened back in 1927 when the building craze was in full swing, the *Cyclone* still managed to outshine most of its contemporaries. Designed by Vernon Keenan and built by Harry Baker, the *Cyclone* has just about

everything a rider could ask for. From its frightfully steep 53-degree first drop to multiple slamming turns and other assorted dives and hops, the fast-paced *Cyclone* perfectly illustrates the compact twister concept.

The *Cyclone* is a wood-track coaster, but it was among the first to employ steel trestlework (along with some wood). That the *Cyclone*'s profile and footprint would be copied in the coaster renaissance period of the late twentieth century is testimony to its tried-and-proven design.

The *Cyclone* itself has been overhauled numerous times during nearly three quarters of a century in service, but it still maintains the rough-and-tumble, streetwise character people have come to know and love. For a time early in the 1970s, it appeared the ride was going to be torn down; instead, it achieved National Historic Landmark status. While the *Thunderbolt* sits nearby in forgotten loneliness and all other Coney classics have faded into memory, the *Cyclone* still rules the beach and boardwalk, roaring proudly into the next millennium.

CYCLONE RACER—The Pike, Long Beach, California: The breathtaking *Cyclone Racer* was the only *Bobs*-style racing coaster designed by Fred Church. Built atop a pier on the California coast, it was the star attraction of an amusement district known as The Pike. The *Cyclone Racer* opened in May 1930 to rave reviews.

Standing almost 100 feet tall, the *Cyclone Racer* was an imposing structure. A double-track racer, each "side" traversed a 3,400-foot circuit for a total route length of nearly 7,000 feet. The layout was packed with steep drops, both flat and swoop turns, and trackage that weaved in and out of the dense framework. Four five-car trains ran continuously.

The *Cyclone Racer* was especially popular (and convenient) with Hollywood filmmakers, and the ride showed up in many movies—notably the 1950s sci-fi classic *Beast from 20,000 Fathoms*—and in TV shows, among them an episode of *Leave it to Beaver*.

As Long Beach sought to upgrade its image in the late 1960s, those in power decided that the "World's Greatest Ride" did not fit in with the city's new agenda. Despite public outrage, the *Cyclone Racer* was reduced to rubble in September 1968. Though Long Beach tried to recapture its glory by bringing in the *Queen Mary* and *Spruce Goose*, the loss of the *Cyclone Racer* will remain a blemish on the city's historical reputation.

CYCLONE—Puritas Springs Park, West Cleveland, Ohio: This wicked creation, opened in 1928, came from the mind of master designer John Miller and is often considered among the most intense of the golden-age coasters that survived the Depression—and certainly designer Miller's most notorious, considering his penchant more "family oriented" rides.

The *Cyclone*'s station sat precariously on the very edge of a deep ravine that traversed the park. The *Cyclone*'s alarmingly steep first drop plunged over the station roof into the valley. After an abrupt pullout, the trains leapt from the ravine and raced through a series of Miller-esque camelback hills. After a quick turnaround, the train unexpectedly dipped down a small hill and then, without warning, plummeted back into the ravine, all the way to the bottom where the track rested right on the valley

CONEY ISLAND *TORNADO* (BOBS)

A *Tornado* train in the boarding process not long before the ride was closed in the mid-1970s. *Michael Boodley*

floor. This was the longest drop on the entire ride and it earned the *Cyclone* a place of honor among the greats.

The Puritas Springs *Cyclone*'s notorious reputation was not merely urban legend. Detailed newspaper accounts from its time reveal multiple incidents in which riders were injured by the violent motion of the ride. The *Cyclone* was even condemned for a short period while adjustments were made. It operated until 1958 and will be remembered forever as an extreme ride in every sense of the word. Remains of this legend can still be found in the forested ravines where Puritas Springs once stood.

***TORNADO* (a.k.a., *Bobs*)—Coney Island, Brooklyn, New York:** Initially known as the *Bobs*, the *Tornado* was yet another jewel in Fred Church's crown. Like the Rye *Airplane* and Riverview *Bobs*, it did not really follow the prescribed *Bobs* pattern. It was a twister, but due to the confined space of the building site, Church had to squeeze a lot into a tight package. The result was a compact, multi-level wonder that deserves to be rebuilt.

Opened in 1926, the Coney *Bobs* was only 71 feet tall, but what Church managed to do with 2,970 feet of track is nothing short of amazing. The ride began with a dank, tunneled approach to the lift hill. As one of the three thickly upholstered trains climbed toward the sky, riders could examine the complicated knot of trackage awaiting them. A curved, almost double-dipping first drop propelled the trains into a maelstrom. Even in examining the few photographs and home movies that exist of this ride, it's difficult to trace the convoluted acrobatics of its trains.

By the dawn of the 1970s, Coney Island was slipping into urban squalor. Though the *Cyclone* was holding its own, Steeplechase was gone, the *Thunderbolt* was in decline, and the *Tornado* was doomed. Several fires of mysterious origin closed the ride and eventually led to its removal in 1978. *Tornado* devotees lament its destruction. Those who prefer its endless turns and curious charm to the steep suicidal plunges of its neighbor often say that the wrong Coney roller coaster was razed.

WILDCATS—Lakeside Park, Dayton, Ohio; Idora Park, Youngstown, Ohio; and Rocky Springs, Lancaster, Pennsylvania: The Philadelphia Toboggan Company built a large number of roller coasters during the golden age, but some members of its *Wildcat* series tend to stand out among others. This radical line of thrillers was introduced to compete with the extravagant creations coming from Fred Church, Harry Baker, and Harry Traver. These three PTC *Wildcats*, all designed by Herbert Schmeck and all featuring different track plans, were a departure from the norm, yet truly exceptional examples of roller coaster wizardry.

IDORA *WILDCAT*

Construction is nearly complete on the new *Wildcat* coaster at Idora Park in Youngstown, Ohio. As built, the ride was riddled with tunnels. Also, in this view looking toward the lift hill (center background), the twisting first drop is visible. Later this was rebuilt into a more traditional straight drop off a flat turnaround, but the ride remained notoriously brutal—and therefore a favorite of coaster connoisseurs. *PTC*

The Lakeside *Wildcat* was built in 1930 on the site of an earlier Ingersoll coaster called the *Derby Racer*. The *Wildcat* began with a long tunnel and a twisted first drop. Numerous low-level "speed hills," mid-course tunnels, and a couple of swoop turns made this "cat" one ferocious animal. Common are the tales of rocketing trains throwing off sparks as they tore through the savage bends and a hidden helix finale (see pages 84–85).

In the same vein of extreme coastering was the Rocky Springs *Wildcat*. This ride utilized portions of the 1918-built John Miller *Jack Rabbit*. The new coaster opened in 1928 and was an immediate hit. Schmeck utilized the previous ride's 500-foot-long tunnel, which turned out of the station and sent trains plowing into the ravine over which the *Wildcat* was built. At the bottom, trains turned sharply and engaged the lift hill. After a 180-degree left turn above the trees and station, the *Wildcat*'s ride really began. The first drop was a steep, 90-foot fall that jogged to the left. A wrenching pullout, followed by a swoop turn (later flattened), three more drops, and a pair of turns within the structure left riders breathless and windblown. Many consider this the most intense of PTC's *Wildcats*.

Opened in 1930, the Idora *Wildcat* likewise began with a long tunnel. As originally built—and like its Lakeside cousin—the first drop twisted in its decent. Later this was rebuilt into a more-traditional flat turnaround off the lift hill that led to the first drop. A speed bump after the first drop threw riders up against the lap bar and hurled them into a wicked fan curve that was famous for cracking ribs—quite literally. Among the various drops and turns that followed was a section of angled straight track that horrified riders into thinking the ride had partially collapsed. Idora Park closed in the 1980s not long after the *Wildcat* was partially burned in an unfortunate welding mishap. Sadly, this spectacular coaster never recovered but is still consistently ranked as one of the ten best golden-age coasters to survive into the renaissance era.

continued from page 45

done with track so heavily banked that it was nearly perpendicular to the ground. The untamed nature of the *Cyclone*s caused passengers to struggle to remain upright, and broken collar bones, fractured ribs, and other injuries were common. A nurse was kept on duty at the Crystal Beach installation to tend to fainting and injured *Cyclone* riders.

Traver's *Cyclone*s debuted at a time when the public accepted such violence in amusement attractions. And though there were indeed documented injuries on some of these early thrill rides, the publicity generated by those incidents caused a rather surprising degree of interest and curiosity. Crowds filled the parks to see what all the excitement was about.

Though these four Traver coasters were extreme in every sense of the word, they were quite popular— but only for a short time. Eventually crowds watching the *Cyclone*s began to outnumber those waiting to ride. Ridership began to plummet (pun intended) while insurance premiums soared on account of injuries. In addition, the unforgiving nature of the steel structure combined with the intense forces generated by heavy trains slamming through the radical track layout made maintenance costly and ongoing.

SHELLPOT COASTER

Philadelphia Toboggan Company was the most prolific coaster-building firm of the golden age. PTC rides showed up coast to coast at parks that were both well-known and obscure. This is the coaster at Shellpot Park, Wilmington, Delaware, circa 1925. *Philadelphia Toboggan Coasters*

BELMONT PARK *CYCLONE*

PTC influence went beyond U.S. borders. Belmont Park near Montreal, Quebec, opened its Schmeck-designed PTC coaster in 1924. Known later as the *Cyclone*, it is shown in 1978 not long before the park closed. *Mike Schafer*

The outrageous rides thus operated for only a few seasons. Crystal Beach's *Cyclone* lasted the longest—until 1945—and only because the owners couldn't afford to dismantle it. Instead, park management called in Herb Schmeck from the Philadelphia Toboggan Company to reinforce the structure enough to keep it running. Finally, in 1947 the Crystal Beach *Cyclone* was replaced with a less-punishing ride called the *Comet*, which, ironically, was built using much of the *Cyclone*'s steel structural components.

The Traver *Cyclone*s are generally considered to have been the most extreme roller coasters ever constructed, and the few films, photos, and actual riders' written accounts of them all substantiate this quite clearly. The fact that these rides all had relatively brief life spans is a fairly good indicator that they were too wild, even for a period in American history that readily accepted violent coasters.

Even after his company went out of business and no one was buying his steel *Cyclone*s, Harry Traver went back to building *Bobs* coasters for Fred Church and remained involved in numerous amusement industry and other ventures in America and abroad until his death in 1961. In any case, Harry Traver has earned a place of honor as a thrill-ride pioneer.

Philadelphia Toboggan Company

The Philadelphia Toboggan Company opened in 1904 in Germantown, Pennsylvania, and was originally known for its toboggan slides and exquisite

PTC'S *GIANT COASTER*

PTC did a lot of renovation and alteration-type work to several coasters over the years, some of them PTC rides and some having been built by other manufacturers. In 1932, Herbert Schmeck did alteration work on Paragon Park's *Giant Coaster* at Hull, Massachusetts. This ride was designed and built by John Miller/PTC in 1917 and is shown in 1979. Now known as the *Wild One*, this excellent ride today resides near Washington, D.C. *Mike Schafer*

51

THE *ATOM SMASHER*

This view from the front seat of the *Atom Smasher* coaster at Rockaway's Playland, Queens, New York, has been seen by millions of people, both for real and vicariously through the famous Cinerama movie system that was the rage in the early 1950s. For the movie *This is Cinerama*, motion-picture cameras were mounted on one of the trains and a trip through the whole ride—one of the more convoluted coasters around—was recorded. A three-projection system and a three-sided screen surrounded the audience and put them *into* the scene. Viewers felt as though they were actually riding the coaster, subconsciously reacting to the train's curves and plunges. The *Atom Smasher* was designed by Vernon Keenan (of nearby Coney Island *Cyclone* fame) and built by National Amusement Device in 1939. Until the ride's closing in 1985, its entrance had a sign denoting it to be "The Cinerama Coaster." As such, the *Atom Smasher* was probably NAD's best-known coaster. *Mike Schafer*

carousels with hand-carved wooden animals. Among the various amusement devices manufactured by PTC, which is still in business, the approximately 140 wooden roller coasters—most of them constructed during the golden age—are counted among its greatest achievements.

The roster of early designers who worked for PTC at one time or another includes John Miller, Joe McKee, and Frank Hoover; but it was Herbert Schmeck who really turned PTC into a powerhouse during the golden age. Though Schmeck originally worked as an apprentice under John Miller, he eventually came into his own and was responsible for some of PTC's most celebrated rides. The firm's many *Wildcat*-series coasters were created to compete with the extreme rides that Fred Church and Harry Traver were creating. Some of PTC's most notables were the *Wildcat*s at Rocky Springs in Lan-

caster, Pennsylvania; Lakeside Park in Dayton, Ohio; and Idora Park in Youngstown, Ohio. Though all now defunct, these rides are symbols of the untamed, freewheeling nature of this period in the roller coaster's colorful history.

The Philadelphia Toboggan Company produced a number of other rides and games of skill (Skee-Ball perhaps being the best-known) during its long history. It even secured the rights to build Norman Bartlett's unusual *Flying Turns* bobsled-style coaster (sidebar). Though several such rides were proposed, PTC, hampered by the Depression, built only one moderately successful installation, the *Flying Turns* at Rocky Point, Warwick, Rhode Island.

PTC managed to survive the Depression and keep the industry supplied with whatever amusements parks could afford until times improved. It was PTC's John Allen who effectively bridged the gap between the first Golden Age and the advent of the second boom in the roller coaster's popularity in 1972. Allen worked extensively with Schmeck in the 1940s and eventually went on to become the company's president. Allen would design of some of PTC's most famous later rides, including the Kings Island (Ohio) *Racer*, which would launch a coaster renaissance.

Though PTC stopped designing roller coasters when John Allen died in 1979, the legacy lives on. A large number of PTC's woodies are still in operation and as popular as ever.

Now headed by longtime employee Tom Rebbie, PTC recently relocated to a larger facility in Hatfield, Pennsylvania. The company, now known as Philadelphia Toboggan Coasters, remains the world's largest supplier of roller coaster vehicles—now including steel-track coaster trains—and related devices.

National Amusement Device

Also known as the Dayton Fun House & Riding Device Company, NAD was established by Aurel Vaszin in the 1920s and became a major player, especially during the dark days of the Great Depression. With the input of Philadelphia Toboggan Company's John Miller in its early years, NAD eventually became one of PTC's chief rivals. Though not nearly as prolific as PTC, NAD's rides and invaluable contributions to the amusement industry, especially in the field of roller coaster design, were exemplary.

While keeping things in line at NAD, founder Vaszin also managed Forest Park near his factory in Dayton. A cheerful and well-liked individual, Vaszin even operated an impressive out-and-back wooden coaster at Forest Park. Some of NAD's best-known rides of the golden era included the *Coaster* (a.k.a. *Atom Smasher*) at Rockaway's Playland in Queens, New York, and Sterling's *Million Dollar Coaster* at Rocky Glen Park, Moosic, Pennsylvania. Perhaps NAD's most recognized contribution to the world of roller

ROLLER COASTERS ✪✪✪✪✪✪✪✪✪ GREAT REVENUE GETTERS!

NATIONAL'S ROLLER COASTER
Roller Coaster 2400 feet long, 68 feet high with 9 dips, every one to the ground. Sensational Ride—Good Repeater—Smooth Ride—100% Safe—Cars Locked in the Track—Passengers Locked in the Car. Safe Construction throughout the Entire System.

ECONOMY ROLLER COASTER
Two different views of our Economy Roller Coaster, gracefully designed. 1400 feet long, 40 feet high, fabricated of 4" tubing, 3 x 4 angle iron for leger. All Braces are made of 2" tubing. The only wood material in this Coaster is the track. This Coaster is absolutely free of maintenance.

TOTAL COST IS FROM $65,000.00 to $70,000.00 DEPENDING ON THE LOCATION AND THE PREVAILING COSTS OF LOCAL CONSTRUCTION AT THE TIME INSTALLATION IS MADE.

NATIONAL AMUSEMENT DEVICE Company
Box 488 VAF
DAYTON, OHIO
Phone: AMherst 3-2646

NAD TRAIN

Probably NAD's most significant contribution to coasterdom were its classic Century Flyer trains. They were (and are) a fixture on many coasters, even those not built by NAD. This brightly colored NAD train is making a test run over the *Zephyr* at Pontchartrain Beach park near New Orleans. *Chuck Davis*

NAD CATALOG

There was a time when one could buy just about anything from a Sears catalog, but a roller coaster probably wasn't one of them. However, there were catalogs from which prospective buyers could select the coaster of their choice. One of the pages from NAD's four-page catalog from the early 1950s featured standard and "economy" coasters. *Scott Rutherford collection*

ZEPHYR AT NEW ORLEANS

Designed by Ed Vettel in 1938, the *Zephyr* was classic L-shaped out-and-back ride flanked by palm trees and splashed with generous doses Art Deco elegance. The *Zephyr* ruled the shores of Lake Pontchartrain until 1983 when the park it called home closed forever. *Otto P. Dobnick*

SANTA CRUZ'S *GIANT DIPPER*

Using Fred Church patents, the *Giant Dipper* was designed by Arthur Looff and opened in 1924. To this day, the *Dipper* remains arguably one of the most meticulously maintained and smooth-riding wooden coasters on the planet. This wonderful ride has been designated a National Historic Landmark and should be at the top of any serious enthusiast's must-ride list. *Otto P. Dobnick*

coasters is the firm's Art Deco–inspired rolling stock. Dubbed Century Flyers, these wood-framed, aluminum-shrouded beauties mimic the sleek streamlined passenger trains of the 1930s and 1940s. Their shiny silver bodies are accentuated by a number of design details, especially the headlighted fronts.

NAD's Century Flyer rolling stock can still be found on many coasters, notably on the *Thunderbolt* at Pittsburgh's Kennywood Park, the *Big Dipper* at Geauga Lake near Cleveland, both coasters at Camden Park near Huntington, West Virginia, and the *Blue Streak* in Conneaut Lake Park at Conneaut Lake, Pennsylvania. In the late 1990s, the *Blue Streak*'s train was completely refurbished and its "headlights" made to actually operate, but it still exemplifies a period in roller coaster design and construction when style and flare meant as much as the spectacular action of the ride itself.

Coaster-building Families

The pioneering Vettel clan, headed by Erwin and Edward A. Vettel, entered the amusement business in

The Flying Turns

Former World War I Canadian Royal Air Force pilot Norman Bartlett worked briefly with John Miller in the late 1920s to introduce the first *Flying Turns* at Lakeside Park in Dayton, Ohio. Opened in 1929, the ride featured small, aluminum, bullet-shaped vehicles equipped with hard rubber wheels set on casters. The ride's "track" was in fact a large trough fashioned of long strips of laminated cypress wood attached to a steel frame. This track was in turn supported by standard coaster trestlework.

With passengers sitting toboggan-style (one in front of the other), the cars were hoisted up a lift hill that looked much like a standard coaster lift hill and released into the trough track. During their freewheeling, unchecked descent, the vehicles gained a remarkable amount of momentum, flying through the tight turns, continuously running up and around the heavily banked curves like a real bobsled. Many found the experience quite frightening, and it was not uncommon for operators to keep a supply of dry seat cushions on hand.

Although the Depression was in full swing, park owners who could afford new rides took advantage of the potential of this great new coaster idea. (Some coaster historians speculate that, had it not been for the Depression, many more *Flying Turns* would have been constructed.) Larger variations of the

FLYING TURNS, CENTURY OF PROGRESS, CHICAGO
Judging by the expressions on riders' faces, this new coastering concept of the Depression era is a hit. This *Flying Turns* was the smallest one built and originally appeared at the "Century of Progress" World's Fair in Chicago in 1939. After the fair, the ride was moved next door to the *Bobs* at Chicago's Riverview Park where it operated until 1967. *Charlie Jacques collection*

Flying Turns found their way into parks such as Euclid Beach (Cleveland), Rocky Point (Rhode Island), Coney Island (New York), and Forest Park (St. Louis). These later versions used trains instead of single vehicles for increased capacity and stability.

The Euclid Beach *Flying Turns* was probably the best-known of Bartlett's ingenious coaster mutant, perhaps because of its large size. However, the infamous *Lake Placid Bobsled*, which opened in 1937 at famed Palisades Park in Fort Lee, New Jersey, joins Harry Traver's steel *Cyclone* triplets as a contender for the title of the most terrifying coaster rides ever operated. This ferocious coaster was notorious for its violent, out-of-control nature. Numerous modifications and constant attempts to tame the ride were made, but it was dismantled in 1946 due to rider complaints, low patronage, and excessive maintenance.

The last *Flying Turns* to survive were those at Riverview Park and Euclid Beach, and each died with those parks in 1967 and 1969 respectively. This unusual type of coaster has an almost cult-like following among coaster enthusiasts, which may in part be why modern versions began to resurface in the 1980s (chapter 5). Though the newer rides offer a somewhat watered-down version of the original, they are still certainly entertaining attractions. Those manufactured by Mack are considered to be closest to the original in terms of ride experience.

LAKESIDE PARK, DENVER

Denver's jewel is Lakeside Park, a magnificent holdover of the great Art Deco era. Located only a few blocks from rival Elitch Gardens' old site (each park's coasters could be seen from their respective lift hills), Lakeside is home to the wonderful Vettel-designed *Cyclone*, shown in 1996 basking in a golden Colorado sunset. The *Cyclone* opened in 1940 and thus can be considered a tribute to the golden age of roller coasters, which would end with the onset of World War II. *Otto P. Dobnick*

LAKESIDE RACING COASTER

Lakeside's mammoth *Derby Racing Coaster* occupied what would become the site of the *Cyclone*. This postcard view is believed to have been taken from Lakeside's landmark tower seen in the upper right of the above photo. *Scott Rutherford collection*

7304. Derby Racing Coaster, Lakeside Park, Denver.

which once ruled the midway at enchanting Pontchartrain Beach near New Orleans.

Luckily, some Vettel-designed coasters are still in operation today: the recently revitalized Conneaut *Blue Streak*; the sensual Art Deco *Cyclone* at Lakeside Park in Denver; and, of course, a portion of the world-famous *Thunderbolt* at Kennywood Park (chapter 4).

Another prominent family that made a significant impact on the development of the American wooden roller coaster was the Loofffs, Charles (a famous carousel carver) and Arthur, of California. Arthur's enormous *Blue Streak*, built on the Santa Monica Pleasure Pier in 1916, was a landmark in the Venice area for many years. Furthermore, Arthur's *Giant Dipper* roller coaster, opened in 1925 at Santa Cruz, California, was designed using Fred Church patents. Arguably the best-maintained wooden coaster in existence, the *Dipper* is still thrilling riders today.

Similarly important was the Pearce family—another example of generations carrying on the tradition of creating fun. More than 30 wooden coasters can be attributed to various members of the Pearce family. The patriarch of the clan, Josiah Pearce, began in 1902 at Pennsylvania's Exposition Park and then branched out, leaving the family's mark on the industry with such notable rides as the now-dormant *Big Dipper* at Ohio's Chippewa Lake Park, and the Pearce's crowning achievement, the incredible *Trip Thru the Clouds*, which opened at Riverview Park in Detroit in 1915. This massive ride was over one mile long and 90 feet tall and reportedly was able to run an amazing six trains simultaneously.

Golden Age in Twilight

The coaster-building craze reached an all-time zenith in 1928, when nearly 40 major roller coasters were constructed at parks around the country. During

the 1890s, working for Pittsburgh-based T. M. Harton Company. At first they concentrated on the installation of the popular figure-8 side-friction rides, acting as contractors for Harton in the field; they built rides all over the U.S. and Canada. The Vettels, like other designers, had their own unique style and passed it on to the succeeding generations, who remained quite active in the family business of building roller coasters.

As the coaster wars heated up, the Vettels spread out to parks around the country to build coasters. Some examples of the family's work include the *Dips* and *Racing Whippet* at West View Park near Pittsburgh (closed in 1978) and the sadly missed *Zephyr*,

EUCLID BEACH *FLYING TURNS*

Euclid Beach's *Flying Turns* coaster opened in 1930 and towered over most other park rides, including the adjacent *Thriller* and *Racing Coaster*. This postcard from the era cleverly shows a cutaway of the trough track to reveal how the ride works. *Scott Rutherford*

PALISADE'S *LAKE PLACID BOBSLED*

The most notorious of the *Flying Turns*-format rides was the *Lake Placid Bobsled* at New Jersey's Palisades Park. It is shown shortly after its construction in 1937. *PTC*

virtually the entire decade of the 1920s, it seemed that good times would last forever for the multitude of amusement parks—and their spectacular roller coaster offerings—that flourished from coast to coast. It was truly a golden age in many ways.

The seemingly carefree and extravagant days of the Roaring Twenties came to a swift and screeching halt with the stockmarket crash of 1929, and the ensuing Great Depression cooled the coaster fever that had swept through the country. The golden age of the roller coaster gave way to an atmosphere of gloom and desperation as the U.S. economy plunged into a tailspin. By the dawn of the 1930s, the buoyant sense of unbridled optimism that had pervaded the previous decade quickly burned itself out as many people simply struggled to survive.

It is estimated that by this time as many as 2,000 wooden roller coasters had been constructed. But the arrival of the Depression found the general public with very little extra cash to keep the abundance of pleasure parks in business. This abrupt downturn in the economy, along with numerous other contributing factors, wounded the amusement industry immeasurably. The once-lucrative business of creating fun was destined for hard times.

After the 1930 season, only a few of the coasters which had already been planned were actually built and put into service. Few other new rides were added as attendance at parks across the country plummeted drastically. During this dark period, many amusement parks were demolished or sold piece by piece when patrons could no longer afford to support them. Others were simply boarded up and abandoned, while owners and investors wrote them off as losses and went in search of new ventures.

During the worst years of the Depression, many park owners were sympathetic to loyal customers. Well aware that most people had little money to spend on rides or games, they often offered free entertainment like outdoor concerts and playground equipment for children, as well as reduced rates on admission to the parks' public swimming pools and dance halls. This practice naturally drew people to the parks, where they would usually spend as much as they could afford to. This was a beneficial diversion, since it actually gave people a diversion that provided

Flying Turns, Euclid Beach Park, Cleveland, Ohio

a brief respite from the dire situation that engulfed the nation—indeed, the world.

Fortunately, coaster-building individuals and firms like National Amusement Device and the Philadelphia Toboggan Company remained in business during the Depression. Though they only built a few new coasters and other rides between them, they still managed to hang on until the bad times grew better. Obviously, money and raw materials were not as abundant has they had been during the 1920s, but investors and park owners determined to offer new attractions found the means to do so. A review of some of the rides put into service during this period illustrates that, even though the sheer number of installations decreased, quality and creativity for those attractions that did open was not spared. In that sense, the golden age was not quite over.

Among the many designers active during these rocky years was the incomparable John Miller. He contributed to a vast number of new coasters and even built a pair of his own unique *Triple Racing Coasters* in 1936 at Fontaine Ferry, Louisville, Kentucky, and State Fair Park, Dallas, Texas. With various

Aerial View, Palisades Amusement Park, Palisades, N.J.

partners, Norman Bartlett constructed numerous examples of his amazing *Flying Turns* at parks around the world.

PTC continued to build wonderful coasters as well—most of them designed by its own Herbert Schmeck—at Idora Park, Youngstown, Ohio (the *Wildcat*, 1930); Lakeside Park, Dayton, Ohio (the *Wildcat*, 1930); Lakewood Park, Waterbury, Connecticut (its name then is unknown, but Schmeck would supervise the move of this ride in 1933 to Canobie Lake, New Hampshire, where today it operates as the *Yankee Cannonball*); Kennywood Park, West Mifflin, Pennsylvania (*Little Dipper*, 1936); Coney Island, Ohio (*Clipper*, 1937); Idlewild Park, Ligioner, Pennsylvania (known today as *Rollo Coaster*, 1938); Port Arthur Pleasure Pier, Port Arthur, Texas (*Comet*, 1940); and Forest Park Highlands, St. Louis, Missouri (*Comet*, 1941).

Prior & Church opened numerous coasters—most of them of

DOWN AT PALISADES PARK

This famed park, made famous by song ("Palisades Park" by Freddy Cannon in 1962) and coaster, had two *Cyclones*. When the Traver "Giant *Cyclone* Safety Coaster" was leveled in 1934, the park's resident wood Miller coaster acquired the *Cyclone* name. That same year, that ride was heavily reworked by Joseph McKee into the classic that became the centerpiece of this beautiful park, as shown in this postcard scene. *B. Derek Shaw collection*

ALPS COASTER, WILLOW GROVE PARK, PHILADELPHIA

Although new coaster construction slowed during the Depression era, PTC's Herbert Schmeck did alteration work on some coasters. In 1939 he reworked the park's venerable scenic railway-type coaster, the *Alps*, shown here with PTC cars that have received some avant garde styling. *PTC*

STERLING'S ROCKY GLEN PARK, MOOSIC, PA.

MIDWAY SCRANTON AND WILKES BARRE

COMET AT PLEASURE PARK, PORT ARTHUR, TEXAS

Located at the now-defunct Pleasure Pier in Port Arthur, Texas, the 1942-built *Comet* is considered one of the best wooden coasters ever to grace the Lone Star State. Designed by PTC's Herb Schmeck, this 75-foot tall, 3, 300-foot-long ride featured several unique low-lying speed hills which produced numerous instances of sustained airtime and intense lateral G-forces. A savage hurricane swept in off the Gulf of Mexico in 1957, silencing the *Comet* forever. *PTC*

THE MILLION DOLLAR COASTER

A rare single-headlight NAD train plunges down the fifth drop on the *Million Dollar Coaster* at Rocky Glen Park, Moosic, Pennsylvania. Designed by Vernon Keenan (of Coney Island *Cyclone* fame) and built by National Amusement Device, this beautiful out-and-back thriller stood 96 feet high and sported an amazing 4,700 feet of track. Sandwiched between the park's lake and the right-of-way of the Lackawanna & Wyoming Valley interurban railway, the *Million Dollar Coaster* (which reportedly cost only $100,000) ruled Rocky Glen's midway until being closed and dismantled in late 1957. *Scott Rutherford collection*

the *Bobs* style— during the Depression era at places such as Playland, Rye, New York (the *Dragon Coaster*, 1929); Cedar Point, Sandusky, Ohio (the *Cyclone*, 1929); Willow Beach, Toledo, Ohio (1929); Forest Park, Genoa, Ohio (1929); Waukesha Beach, Pewaukee, Wis. (the *Bobs*, 1929); and The Pike, Long Beach, California (the *Cyclone Racer*, 1930). Interestingly, the Waukesha Beach *Bobs* bore a strong resemblance to the famed *Aeroplane Dips* coaster that had been built at Rye in 1928.

Other notable coasters given life at this time include the NAD/Keenan-designed *Coaster* (renamed *Atom Smasher* after World War II) at Rockaway's Playland, Queens, New York (1933) and the *Million Dollar Coaster* at Rocky Glen, Moosic, Pennsylvania (1945). The Vettel family was responsible for rides at

Conneaut Lake Park near Meadeville, Pennsylvania (the *Blue Streak*, 1938); Pontchartrain Beach Park, New Orleans, Louisiana (the *Zephyr*, 1938); and Lakeside Park, Denver, Colorado (*Cyclone*, 1940).

Even though times were indeed tough, the parks that managed to survive this era of waning can directly attribute their longevity to the roller coaster. Among the handful of rides built between 1929 and 1945 that thrive as this book went to press are Conneaut's *Blue Streak*; Lakeside's

Cyclone; the *Zipper* (later, *Cyclone*) at Williams Grove, Mechanicsburg, Pennsylvania; and Playland's *Dragon Coaster*. These extraordinary examples of roller coaster technology should be regarded as cherished symbols of our recreational heritage.

The Depression marked the waning years of the golden age of roller coasters, and the start of World War II signaled the end of that marvelous epoch. The count fluctuated during the Depression as many parks closed for good while a few parks built new rides as noted. But during the war itself, few if any coasters opened. PTC, for example, didn't build any coasters nor did it undertake any major alteration work to existing rides during 1942, 1943, and 1944.

Although the close of World War II brought unprecedented optimism and growth to America, that did not necessarily translate to good times for coasters. The roller coaster was still in for a bumpy ride— but with a surprise ending.

THE *SKY ROCKET*, NORFOLK, VIRGINIA

A fully loaded train on the *Sky Rocket* at Ocean View Amusement Park just prior to the start of World War II. Ocean View was a favorite haunt of service personnel due its proximity to nearby military installations. During the conflict, parks often treated serviceman in uniform to complementary perks as a means to boost public morale. *Scott Rutherford collection*

THE *BLUE STREAK*, CONNEAUT LAKE, PENNSYLVANIA

The rambunctious *Blue Streak* tucked away in the woods of northwestern Pennsylvania is a must ride for coaster lovers. The steep drops of these golden-age classic are some of the best around. *Mike Schafer*

3

Nuts and Bolts

How Coasters Work

MISTER TWISTER, ELITCH GARDENS, DENVER

The world-class coaster of Denver's old Elitch Gardens (the park moved to a new location in 1995), the rip-roaring *Mister Twister*—later known simply as *Twister*—illustrates the basics of coaster construction: a track support system, track, and coaster vehicles. The means of propulsion once the coaster vehicles are off the lift hill is free and lots of it is readily available: gravity. In this 1983 scene, a *Twister* train is hurtling through the ride's famed high-speed helix; just seconds later, the same train will have circled around and be blasting past on the foreground track. *Mike Schafer*

Generally, there are a great number of misconceptions about how roller coasters actually work: What powers the trains? What keeps the cars from jumping the tracks? How do the brakes function?

To begin, there are two basic types of roller coasters: the classic wood-track rides and those sporting track fashioned of steel. As will become apparent, the track construction itself—not the track supporting structure—defines the category into which a coaster is placed.

To confuse matters, many wood-track coasters have a steel support structure or a combination of wood and steel. By the same token, a few steel coasters have

wood support structurework beneath those tubular steel rails. But in essence, if the track is made of laminated wood on which steel strap rails are mounted, it's considered a wood coaster. If the track is made entirely of steel components, it's a steel coaster.

A View of Scenic Railway and Ball Grounds, Euclid Beach, Cleveland, Ohio.

SCENIC RAILWAY TRACK

Switchback coasters and *Scenic Railways* almost always employed traditional railroad-type track, with "T" rails and flanged-wheel cars, as illustrated in this view of the *Scenic Railway* at Cleveland's Euclid Beach. Dips had to be gentle, and curves had to be negotiated at reasonable speed (*Scenic Railway* coasters usually had brakemen aboard the trains to control speed) because cars were not locked to the track. In this scene, a train is being hoisted to the top of the lift hill with a cable rather than a chain. A gripper device on the trains, manually operated by the brakeman, caught and gripped the continuously moving cable—the same arrangement utilized by cable-car street railway systems such those in San Francisco. *B. Derek Shaw collection*

Today there are numerous variations and combinations of each type of ride, but virtually all roller coasters are slaves to one very common attribute: gravity. The roller coaster is a perfect illustration of the simple concept that what goes up will, in all likelihood, eventually come down. On a roller coaster, this usually occurs quite rapidly, and that's a major reason why we ride the things in the first place. For purposes of this book, we define a roller coaster as any wheeled entertainment device operating on a fixed guideway course and propelled primarily by means of gravity and momentum.

Mechanically, all modern roller coasters are incredibly complex machines. Included here are descriptions that may help the novice thrillseeker understand just what makes these towering scream machines tick.

The Evolution of Tracking

Most of the earliest American coasters—namely the switchback-type coasters and *Scenic Railways*—

simply employed the tracking method used by railroads: a flanged wheel riding atop an iron or steel rail. Just as on their larger steam-belching cousins, the flange on a coaster car's wheel acted as a natural guide wheel which steered the trains around turns. This arrangement worked fine for the relatively slow-moving, gentle up-and-down rides of that era where most of the track ran a straight-line course, but the flat curves could not be negotiated at high speed without disastrous results. Some other method of tracking had to be devised to keep cars safely on increasingly convoluted layouts.

The answer was the side-friction coaster. This new technology called for coaster cars equipped with flat (i.e., non flanged) steel "tractor" or running wheels to carry the weight of the car, and horizontally mounted "side friction" guide wheels to keep the cars on course. Set at perpendicular angles to and on both sides of the main track were upright boards that formed a wooden channel through which the cars ran. The side-friction wheels made contact with the upright boards through curves and other unconventional maneuvers. This system allowed for increased speed, especially on turns.

The side-friction technology caught on quickly, and soon most coasters, beginning with the Figure-8 rides, were of side-friction design. This allowed for large dips and tight turns without the worry of having cars jump the track. The main drawback to this system was that it did not prevent cars that were moving at high speed from lifting off the track at the apex of a short hill; further, side-friction coasters could be quite jostling due to the amount of play between the side-friction wheels and the track side boards.

Coaster builder John Miller almost single-handedly changed all this with his upstop- or under-friction wheel arrangement—an ingenious design that ushered in the golden age of roller coasters and one which is still employed by virtually all coasters. The upstop wheels and their specially designed track effectively locked the coaster cars to the track and provided the perfect means for taking the wooden roller coaster to much greater levels of terror.

As with side-friction design, Miller employed flangeless tractor wheels to carry the weight of the

car and side-friction wheels to keep it on course. However, Miller fashioned his track of laminated layers of wood planking to form what in essence was an upside-down L-shaped rail that raised the trains high above the "ties" or crossmembers. The side-friction wheels rode against the inside edge of the L-rail. The final ingredient to this mix was the under-friction (upstop) wheels which extended beneath the L-rail. When the car or train entered a low-gravity moment out on the course, riders were treated to some out-of-seat "airtime" but the upstop wheels prevented the cars from completely taking flight.

Though Fred Church and a number of other designers reverted to a flanged-wheel format, they did so with the addition of upstop safety bars (which, like upstop wheels, skidded against the underside of the rail at low-gravity points) for their extreme coasters of the 1920s. Variations of Miller's original upstop wheel system have been incorporated on most all wooden roller coasters; some use rollers rather than full-fledged wheels, for example. Even today's modern steel coasters use a version of Miller's pioneering vision to keep the lightning-fast trains on course and anchored to the track.

SIDE-FRICTION COASTER

This view of the *Giant Coaster* at now-defunct Crystal Beach in southern Ontario illustrates the principle of side-friction design whereby side-mounted wheels on the coaster cars ride against side-friction rails, which are perpendicular to the ground. The horizontal rails merely support the weight of the train while the side-friction rails keep it on course. One of the last surviving side-friction coasters, *Giant Coaster* operated until 1989. *Mike Schafer*

Wood Track

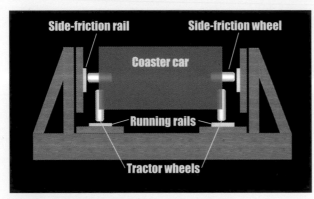

1. SIDE-FRICTION TRACK AND WHEEL ARRANGEMENT

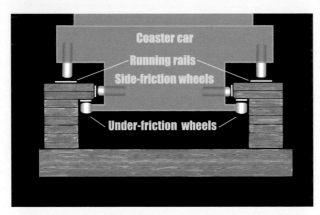

2. STANDARD WOOD-TRACK CONSTRUCTION AND WHEEL ARRANGEMENT

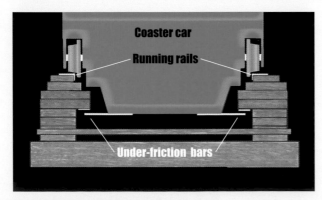

3. FLANGED-WHEEL WOOD-TRACK CONSTRUCTION AND WHEEL ARRANGEMENT

These diagrams show three basic types of wood-track construction and coaster car wheel arrangement.

(1) Although once very common, side-friction track is now virtually non-existent in North America, the most notable surviving example being that on the *Leap The Dips* at Lakemont Park, Altoona, Pennsylvania.

(2) The standard laminated-wood track construction and wheel arrangement used on most wood-track coasters today. The coaster car is shown in a "negative G" situation wherein the tractor wheels are not in contact with the running rail while the upstop or underfriction wheels or rollers are in contact with the underfriction rails to prevent the car from rising completely off the track

(3) A few wood-track coaster trains employ flanged wheels, which eliminate the need for side-friction wheels. On either standard or flanged-wheel coasters with minimal negative Gs, underfriction wheels may be substituted with simple skid bars, as shown in this drawing.

Wood-Track Structure

Though the structure and track arrangement may appear different from one designer to the next, all wooden coasters share important common traits. The track on a wooden roller coaster consists of a parallel series of laminated, or stacked, wooden planks. Depending on the designer's specifications and thickness of the individual boards used, the number of layers can vary from ride to ride. Typically, the laminates consist of seven to nine layers. Although oak was once preferred for track structure due to its strength and longevity, it is expensive and can be difficult to locate. The most popular lumber used for modern tracking is Douglas fir. It more readily accepts the all-important pressure preservation treatment and is able to withstand the brutal pounding delivered by thundering coaster trains.

Tracking a wooden roller coaster is an art form in itself. The process is extremely time-consuming because each individual 12-foot board must be nailed in place foot by foot and slowly bent to conform to the ride's profile using large C-clamps. Once the first layer is down, the second is started, and the process continues until the track bed is complete. Thus, if a ride's track length is measured at 4,000 feet, that includes two laminated rails comprised of up to nine layers of wood each. A simple calculation indicates a mountain of lumber is needed just for the track. Furthermore, a staggering amount of nails and bolts are used to hold the rails together.

Attached with countersunk bolts atop the wooden rails are long lengths of half-inch-thick flat bar stock, usually six inches wide. This is the surface on which the weight-bearing wheels of the trains roll. Also, on most wooden coasters, strips of steel are bolted to the inside and underside of the wooden track. This three-sided steel covering provides a smooth running surface for the train's tractor wheels, horizontal guide wheels, and upstop wheels, respectively. This bar-stock steel, like the layers of wood on which it rests, must be carefully bent to match the angle and radii of the track. Again, this is where the expertise of the trackers is put to the test. Deviations at any point can result in a train becoming stranded due to the track gauge being off.

The track itself is at first attached to a series of thick horizontal wooden ledgers, or cross beams. Numerous gauging ties are interspersed between the ledgers to support the trackside catwalk and maintain the crucial spacing between the rails. Surprisingly, this entire tightly assembled track network is not rigidly attached to the support structure, except in high-stress areas like tight turns or banked track sections. Even though the heavy track virtually floats atop most of the ledgers, its substantial construction, and the fact that it is one long interconnected entity, allows it to maintain its integrity and shape quite well.

A wooden coaster's track is supported by a complex maze of trestlework utilizing "bents." These upright members are usually comprised of a pair of

FLANGED-WHEEL COASTER

The flanged wheels of the vintage Prior & Church trains operating on *Roller Coaster* at the Western Washington Fairgrounds near Puyallup, Washington, are plainly visible in this 1991 scene. *Terry Lind*

CONVERTED SIDE-FRICTION COASTER

The *Jack Rabbit* at now-closed Idora Park in Youngstown, Ohio, was built as a side-friction coaster circa 1920. Once under-friction-wheel technology caught on, the *Jack Rabbit*—like many other side-friction rides—was rebuilt with underfriction track and trains. This scene shows the ride as it appeared in 1983. *Mike Schafer*

COASTER TRACK UNDER CONSTRUCTION

A closeup view of the track construction on the *American Eagle*—a twin-track racing coaster at Great America near Chicago—in 1980 shows laminated-wood track construction. The strap steel rails temporarily draped on the track will be applied to the laminates with flush, countersunk bolts. Also note the bent construction of the raised sections of the ride (on which track has yet to be built) sandwiching the foreground track and compare with the diagram on the facing page. *Mike Schafer*

tall 4 x 6–inch posts set atop concrete pilings approximately nine feet apart. The posts are connected by a diverse collection of cross members and bracing. (This bracing varies according to each designer's building style.) When the required height of the ride exceeds the available length of timbers, they are spliced together, one atop the other, until the necessary elevation is achieved.

The bents are laced together and reinforced by a system of internal and external bracing. On high sections such as the lift hill, tall climbs and on turns, angled batter braces help support the structure and absorb the lateral forces generated by the heavy trains. Sometimes chains, steel cables, or other measures are used to maintain structural integrity.

Coasters that utilize galvanized steel for their support structure are constructed in much the same manner as their all-wood cousins. A few woodies even sport a combination of both materials. Whatever the support materials, as stated previously, it is the laminated wooden track that classifies a roller coaster as wooden instead of steel.

Steel-Track Coasters

Steel coasters offer a more controlled ride experience than the wooden variety. The precision with which they are designed and the tight tolerances applied to steel coaster trains gives steel-track rides a relatively quiet, sanitized flavor, but at the same time it allows for a far more convoluted track plan, complete with vertical loops, barrel rolls, and other acrobatics that are not feasible with wood coaster construction. It also allows for some radical new approaches to coastering: suspended and inverted roller coasters in which the track is above the train.

With the opening of the *Matterhorn Bobsleds* at Disneyland in 1959, the tubular steel track and polyurethane or nylon wheels set the precedent for a brand-new direction for the amusement industry. Steel-track coasters existed before the Matterhorn, but they were basically "kiddie" carnival coasters or *Wild Mouse*–type rides utilizing a flat angle-iron running rail. Not only was this track difficult to bend and shape, it produced a rather noisy and often choppy ride experience.

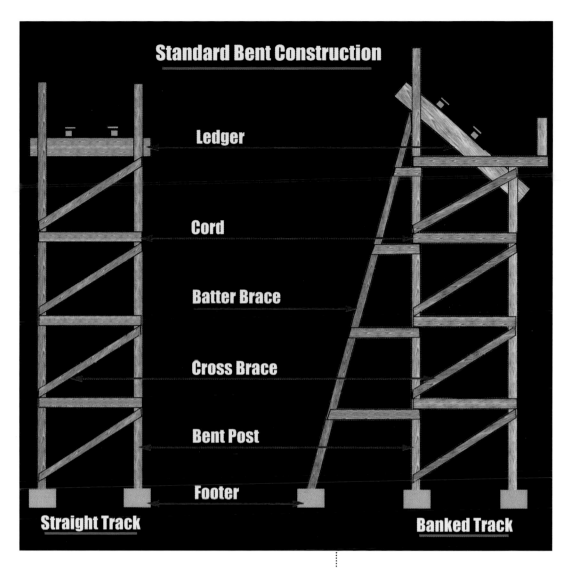

Standard Bent Construction

Ledger

Cord

Batter Brace

Cross Brace

Bent Post

Footer

Straight Track

Banked Track

Arrow Development (today, Arrow Dynamics) was a pioneer in refining tubular steel-track technology. That company's invaluable research and experience with steel coaster construction paved the way for the modern metal thrillers that riders now enjoy. Though others around the world have refined the technology and created their own versions, they all use the same basic concept Arrow devised over 40 years ago: a track made of hollow tubular rails which coaster cars grip with wheel assemblies that include running, side-friction, and upstop wheels coated with a nylon/polyurethane compound. The rails are welded to steel rail-spacing crossmembers and the whole track system likewise is welded to a steel support system or bolted to a wood-support system.

Although modern steel coasters are based on that

BENT CONSTRUCTION

These diagrams illustrate typical bent construction on a coaster with a wood trestle supporting system. Bents under banked curve track generally require batter bracing to counteract the outward forces generated by a coaster train speeding around the curve. Footers are usually poured concrete. *Artwork, Scott Rutherford*

FOOTERS AND BENTS

An overall construction view of the *American Eagle* racing coaster at Great America, Gurnee, Illinois, in 1980 shows bents of treated lumber being raised with a crane in the ride's helix section. Note the batter braces on the outside of the helix structure and the concrete footings in the foreground. Some workers have even begun to apply white paint to the *Eagle*. *Mike Schafer*

AMERICAN EAGLE, COMPLETED

Almost a year after the construction photos were taken, the *American Eagle* stands—finished and in service—in regal splendor on a late summer's night in 1981. The wooden giant has become a landmark along Interstate 94 linking Chicago and Milwaukee. *Mike Schafer*

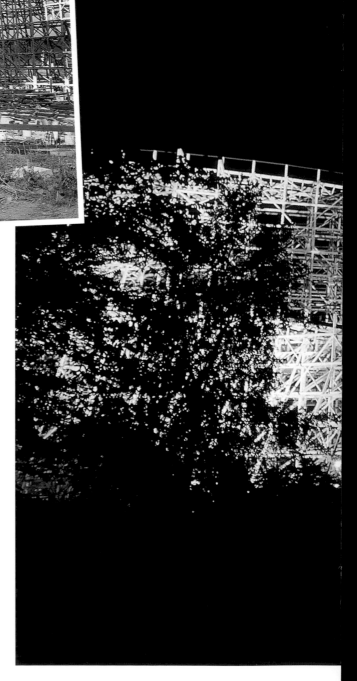

simple concept, there exist numerous and complex variations, depending on what firm is responsible for the design. Supporting structure, too, varies wildly with all-steel coasters. Some steel support systems are similar to those used by all-wood coasters—i.e., a system of bents, crossmembers and bracing, but made of steel rather than wood. Many coaster builders employ a steel pole arrangement which, although it appears minimalistic, is very stable, especially when augmented by guy wires.

Coaster Power

Except for a number of compact steel coasters (Schwarzkopf's *Jumbo Jet*-type coasters, for example) and early "third-rail" (cog-wheel) coasters, there are no motors mounted in the cars themselves. Coaster trains are indeed free-wheeling. However, there has to be some method of getting the trains to the gravity part of their course, and on nearly all roller coasters that is by way of the lift hill, which is almost universally at the beginning of the ride and is the highest point on the ride. The most prevalent means of conveying

WHEEL ASSEMBLY FOR STEEL-TRACK COASTERS

An underside view of *Superman—Ride of Steel* at Six Flags Darien Lake (Darien Center, New York), and the detail diagram at right, show how trains are locked to the track. As with wood-track coaster trains, a combination of tractor or running wheels, side-friction wheels, and under-friction wheels keep coaster trains from launching into outer space. On some steel coasters, the side-friction wheels are positioned on the outside of the rails; on others, it's inside, depending on track construction. *Photo, Scott Rutherford; rendering, Intraxx*

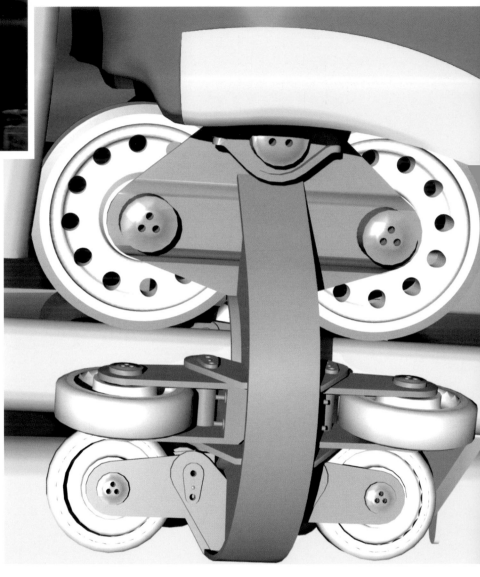

trains to the top of the lift hills is the continuously moving drag chain.

The process works likes this: After the train is loaded and passengers are secured by some type of safety restraint, the station brakes are released and the cars roll by gravity—sometimes assisted by specially mounted trackside tires that are motorized to momentarily grip and propel the train—toward the base of the lift hill. At this point, narrow metal protrusions (called "chain dogs") below two or more of the cars engage the sprockets of the chain, and the train is hoisted up the first hill. After cresting the apex, the train is automatically disengaged from the chain and completes its journey back to the station with only gravity and momentum as the power source. A few coasters feature a second lift hill partway through the course.

Some steel coasters use a tire-driven friction lift system, cables, and even magnetic propulsion (discussed in chapter 6), but the chain lift remains the most popular method. In addition, the sound of a chain lift and chain-dog system creates a certain apprehension for riders as their train clank-clank-clanks ominously up the lift hill.

This gravity factor presents designers with the challenge of using a finite source of energy to provide the most entertaining ride possible. That's where creativity and an understanding of physics, dynamics, and engineering are combined to assure that the train and its passengers comfortably negotiate the

COASTER ENGINEERING
Steel-Track

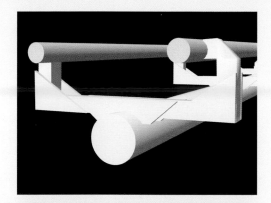

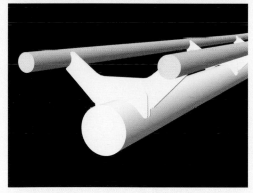

Steel roller coaster track comes in various forms, depending on the respective designer and the type of trains which will be used. Regardless, the track is typically comprised of a central "spine," or beefy carrying tube, to which track ties are affixed. Tubular rails are in turn welded to the "ties" to complete the track system.

The upper diagram is representative of track used by Arrow Dynamics and Vekoma International. The wheel assemblies for this track hug the top, bottom, and insides of the rails.

The lower rendering represents a track that makes use of a wheel assemblies which grab the top, bottom and outside of the rails. Bollinger & Mabillard, Schwarzkopf and most others use variations of this configuration.

layout and return to the unloading platform. There are countless crucial parameters with which designers must contend so that their rides operate consistently and safely under a variety of situations. Varying passenger loads, friction, amount and consistency of wheel lubrication, and wind drag are just some of the circumstances which can and do affect the way a roller coaster behaves on a particular run.

Seasoned riders are well aware how temperamental certain coasters can be, especially wooden rides. The ambient temperature, especially excessive heat and humidity, can dramatically determine the way a coaster train reacts on a given day. Also, a strong wind can act as a natural braking force, should the train encounter the pesky breeze at just the right angle. On taller coasters, especially those located around lakes or oceans, wind speed indicators placed at critical points along the layout are crucial to the ride's operation. These instruments relay pertinent information back to ride operators, who constantly monitor wind gusts in case they reach levels that could negatively interfere with a train's forward momentum.

Rollbacks (a situation in which a coaster train dramatically loses speed and fails to top a hill) due to adverse wind conditions are not uncommon, especially in inverted track sections of looping coasters. Though these situations pose no real danger to riders, they are major headaches for park maintenance crews as guests must be carefully removed from the train and the cars winched over the next hill to complete the circuit.

GEMINI, CEDAR POINT

The *Gemini* racing coaster at Cedar Point, Sandusky, Ohio, is one of a handful of tubular steel-track coasters in North America that employ wood supporting structure for a more traditional look. Built by Arrow Development, *Gemini* opened in 1978. On busy days, six 30-passenger trains can be operated, which makes this ride one of the highest capacity coasters around.
Mike Schafer

CHAIN LIFT

The longtime tried-and-proven method of hoisting coaster trains to the high point of their journey is the chain lift. The chain moves continuously (or is activated upon a train's release from the station) and "chain dogs" on the undersides of coaster cars engage the links of the chain. At the top of the lift hill (this is the crest of the *Tailspin* lift hill at now-razed Dandelion Park, Muskego, Wisconsin), the chain disengages the car as it coils around the chain pulley wheel. From there, gravity takes over. *Mike Schafer*

Depending on the location of the rollback, as well as the ride itself, sometimes the individual cars have to be completely removed from the track with cranes and rerailed back at the loading station.

On the upside of nature's atmospheric shenanigans, riding a roller coaster during a light rain or just after a storm can increase train speed dramatically, especially on wooden coasters. Water gathers on the rails, mixing with oil and grease to form an ultra-slick surface. This friction reduction makes for a zippier trip.

While the majority of the general public will postpone an amusement park visit if inclement weather is forecast, experienced coaster enthusiasts usually seize the opportunity. As long as there is no lightning involved (which will close all outdoor coasters), crowds will be light and the coasters intense.

SELF-PROPELLED LIFT

Some coasters employ a lift-hill system whereby the trains themselves contain small electric traction motors that drive cog wheels which engage in a ratcheted section of track to pull the trains up the lift hill. The principal is much the same as that found in cog railways such as at Pikes Peak, Colorado, and in Europe. By necessity the motors have to be small, which makes it impractical for trains to conquer steep lift hills. Thus, in most cases—as with this *Jumbo Jet* coaster at Cedar Point in 1977—the lift hill trackage has to be arranged in an upward spiraling helix to minimize the grade the trains must climb. All-steel *Jumbo Jet*s and their kin are essentially portable rides, and this one has since been moved to La Feria in Mexico City. *David P. Oroszi*

Safety Devices

Anti-rollbacks: That familiar clanking sound associated with most coasters during the lift hill ascent is caused by a safety device patented by the prolific John Miller back in 1910. Chain dogs, also called "hoisting dogs," not only enable the coaster train to climb the lift hill, they also serve as anti-rollback devices. Basically, the device consists of a pivoting mechanism that latches onto the moving chain during the climb up the lift. A second pivoting safety dog works independently by making contact with a series of ratchets located on the track alongside the chain. This acts as a backup safety measure during the lift sequence as well as near the crests of certain hills out on the course. Should the chain break during a lift, or if a train fails to mount a hill during its circuit, the backward motion of the vehicles will be restricted by the anti-rollbacks, securing the cars in place until the situation can be resolved. Though virtually all lift hills use a version of this ratcheting anti-rollback system, not every coaster features them along the circuit.

Brakes: As the roller coaster progressed from the simple switchback- and *Scenic Railway*-format of the late 1800s to the high-speed wooden and steel coast-

ers we know today, the braking systems devised to slow or stop the trains evolved as well.

Through the mid-1980s, the most common braking systems for wooden coasters were called "skid" or "sled" brakes. These devices involved a series of long, flat parallel bars situated between the running rails. In normal position, these bars were raised so that when the train approached the loading platform, the skid brakes would make contact with brake shoes mounted on the undersides of the cars. The friction created brought the train to a smooth stop, sometimes actually raising it slightly off the rails. Once the train was unloaded and refilled with passengers, the operator lowered the brakes by pulling one or more long wooden brake handles or levers inside the

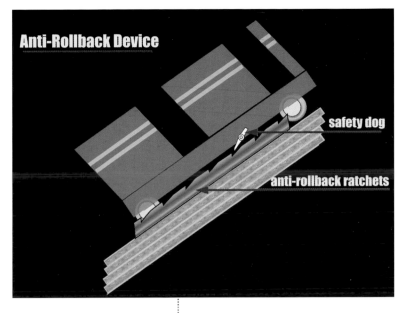

Anti-Rollback Device

safety dog

anti-rollback ratchets

"CHAIN DOGS"

The "clank, clank, clank" that passengers hear as their train slowly surmounts the lift hill of a most coasters is the "safety dog" or anti-rollback safety device. Should the chain break, the safety dogs will engage the anti-rollback ratchets and prevent the train from rolling backward. Anti-rollback ratchets are also found near the tops of other hills on the coaster's course in the event that a train fails to surmount a hill due to lost inertia resulting from extreme wind, wheel failure, or other similar conditions. *Artwork by Scott Rutherford*

SLED OR SKID BRAKES

As the ride operator (in the shadows at left in the photo) leans heavily against the brake lever, a *Dragon Coaster* train at Playland Park, Rye, New York, slows to a halt upon return to the loading station. The wide bars between the rails are the skid brakes, and you can see how they press up against the train's brake pads, which are partially visible below the front of the lead car. *Otto P. Dobnick*

station area. With brakes released, the train coasted out of the station and began its next run.

This manual braking system was obviously reliable, for it was in use for more than a century and can still be found on some rides. Later versions were equipped with air-actuated control levers, replacing the sheer muscle power operators had to use. Skid brakes, however, can be problematic during damp weather if the brake run is not covered by a shed or tunnel. Water collecting on the brakes naturally reduces efficiency. Many veteran riders can probably remember when wet brakes allowed their trains to sail through the station and back out onto the course. These unexpected free rides were rarely unpleasant.

Though another braking system known as the "squeeze brake" was developed for use on some wooden coasters built in the mid–twentieth century, it was the steel coaster (especially the looping rides that came along in the mid-1970s) that benefited from and perfected this style of brake. Also known as a "fin brake," this configuration features long metal fins hanging beneath the train or attached to the cars' lower sides. When these fins pass through pneumatically controlled brake units between the rails (or on the sides of the track), the fins are caught in a tight clamp, effectively and sometimes abruptly bringing the trains to a screeching halt.

Squeeze brakes are now in use on nearly every roller coaster, even the new wooden rides. Some of the older classics have been retrofitted with this modern convenience. Also, within the last few years, a reverse magnetic braking system has begun to show up on high-tech rides. Though these systems require less space and are practically fail-safe, the climactic jolting stop they produce make them far less graceful than the old-fashioned skid brakes.

Though the majority of brakes are located on the final approach and in the station areas, there are sometimes brakes placed at strategic points out on the ride's course. Some of these remote, or "block," brakes are used as emergency safety devices. They are able to bring a coaster train to a complete halt should an incident occur with another train or if operational problems arise. There are also smaller units called "trim brakes" used to control excessive train speed or to maintain proper spacing between multiple trains operating on the same circuit.

Regardless of what type of brake is in use, a fail-safe measure is designed into the system. In default position, the brakes are always on. Only when a force such as compressed air, springs, or old-fashioned brute strength is applied are the brakes disengaged so that trains may pass. In the event of a power failure or loss of air pressure, the brakes thus are set to automatically engage, bringing all trains to a stop at the next full braking location.

While block brakes are a valuable safety measure, at least one contemporary designer insists that, if a roller coaster is properly designed and its construction expertly executed, there is absolutely no reason why trim brakes should ever be required. Most coaster connoisseurs agree with this statement. When a good roller coaster is laced with redundant trim brakes, the main purpose of which is to reduce wear and tear on the ride's structure and trains, the thrill intended by the designer is dramatically lessened. Though this may lower operating costs in the long run, the coasters themselves become tame shadows of their creators' fundamental objective. However, with rising insurance costs and the litigious temperament of modern

FIN BRAKES

The Schwarzkopf-built *Laser* coaster at Dorney Park, Allentown, Pennsylvania, illustrates the fin-brake system that has become widely accepted for both wood and steel coasters. Visible on the stored train at left are horizontal brake fins protruding from the lower sides of the cars. These car-mounted fins are gripped by trackside-mounted squeeze-brake assemblies as illustrated by the arriving train at right. On many coasters, the fins are mounted beneath the cars perpendicular to the track, and the squeeze brakes themselves are mounted between the rails. *Scott Rutherford*

American society, parks have little option but to overly restrain many of their coasters (and riders) to protect themselves from frivolous lawsuits.

Block or safety zone systems: Even before the advent of modern computers, which are now being used to monitor and help control a roller coaster's operation, there existed a safety practice referred to as the "block system." This procedure is similar to the safety zone systems in use on passenger and freight railroads as well as subways worldwide. The objective is to maintain proper spacing between multiple trains operating on the same track.

When the block system was first developed for early high-speed wooden coasters, operators were informed of a particular train's location by a series of electrical limit switches physically tripped by the vehicles as they rolled by. Mechanical relays later gave way to solid state proximity switches and photoelectric sensors. If a train enters the assigned space, or block, of another train, or if it is traveling too fast or too slowly, operators can act accordingly by holding trains in the station or on the chain lift or by activating emergency brakes along the track to temporarily suspend the ride's operation.

With the increased capacity of modern rides, multiple trains are a necessity. Dependable industrial microprocessor computers are common on today's complex coasters. By monitoring all phases of a ride's operation, they keep track of and maintain the correct spacing between all trains, control chain speed, continually check air pressure for the braking system, and even watch to see that lap bars are locked in place.

SAFETY BLOCKING

As with railroads, roller coasters require block systems for multiple-train operation on a single track. This view of *Ninja* at Six Flags St. Louis (Eureka, Missouri), shows a train passing through the ride's intermediate block braking section. If for some reason the train ahead of this one had slowed or stalled in its operating zone, or "block," it would have activated the safety brakes to fully stop the following train in the preceding block. *Ninja* was built in 1986 by Vekoma and Arrow Dynamics for Expo '86 in Seattle and relocated to Six Flags St. Louis in 1989. *Terry Lind*

Though operators have basic control over their rides, their actions must coincide with parameters programmed into the redundant computer system. Human error is always a possibility, but the computer can drastically lower the likelihood of an accident.

Restraints: Early wooden coasters had no substantial type of restraint system. After all, those primitive rides rarely exceeded 12 MPH. However, once speeds began to increase and track configurations became a bit more daring, designers had to develop a way to keep riders inside the cars. A stationary, or fixed, metal lap bar was attached to the inside of the car, and riders slipped beneath it when entering the vehicle. This bar served as a hand hold as well as a restraint. If the ride was a wild one, sometimes a simple leather seat belt was used in conjunction to this static lap bar. Eventually, several similarly functioning types of locking lap bars were developed. The bar was lowered and locked across passengers' laps at the start of the ride and could only be released by an attendant or a device over which the cars passed as they entered the unloading platform. Over the years this system, which became the industry norm, evolved further, and various electrical and mechanical releases were developed.

Due to rising insurance costs and a small number of isolated incidents in which foolish riders managed to squirm out from beneath the lap bars in order to stand up (sometimes with dire consequences), a new individual ratcheting lap bar was developed. This device features a thick, padded lap bar for each rider that adjusts to individual body size. However,

numerous riders favor the traditional lap bar over the ratcheting type, since the latter can be painful on more aggressive rides. Like seat dividers, seat belts, and headrests, this modern lap bar greatly reduces rider movement and therefore deters from the overall coaster experience.

Contemporary steel coasters feature a number of different restraint systems, including the non-intrusive U-shaped ratcheting lap bars that appeared on Schwarzkopf-brand looping coasters in the mid-1970s. American-designed looping coasters came out of the box with a cumbersome over-the-shoulder restraint. Due to overzealous insurance companies and the actions of a few careless riders, various versions of the over-the-shoulder contrivance are now extant on most looping coasters. Curiously, there are still a handful of looping coasters, all Schwarzkopf-designed, that somehow manage to safely thrill millions with only the original lap bar.

Roller Coaster Trains

Roller coaster vehicles come in all shapes, sizes and styles. Many early coasters and some later steel coasters such as the *Wild Mouse* and *Jet Stars*, use individual cars seating between two and four passengers. Traditional coaster cars seat four, six, or eight passengers, with six being the most common. On larger rides of both the wood and steel variety, cars are linked to form trains of varying lengths and passenger capacities. Larger rides usually use two or more trains to increase capacity and keep the queue lines flowing. In fact, some German portable fairground coasters use as many as five seven-car trains, all operating on the same track layout. This type of operation requires split-second timing on the operator's part, as well as an advanced computer system capable of keeping the trains all properly spaced to avoid collisions.

Typically, wood coasters

use a boxy, low-slung collection of cars made of a combination of wood and steel or aluminum, and there have been a few instances of wood-track coaster trains incorporating fiberglass carbodies—though some judge their comfort and ride quality to be inferior to wood-and-steel carbodies. Steel-coaster trains are almost always constructed of fiberglass, steel, and aluminum.

Generally, there are three types of coaster trains: conventional, articulated, and trailer articulated. The cars of a conventional train are coupled together railroad-style and each have their own set of wheels

continued on page 82

Some Classic Coaster Trains

VINTAGE COASTER TRAINS
The number of vintage trains from the first golden age of roller coasters is dwindling as new rolling stock replaces time-worn veterans. Fortunately there are exceptions, among them the colorful 1920s-era trains that were still rolling merrily along on Kennywood Park's wonderful *Jack Rabbit* coaster, shown in this 1991 view, right into the new millennium. *Terry Lind*

PTC also recently entered into the steel-track coaster train market.

The Cadillac of wood-track coaster trains were those manufactured by National Amusement Device (NAD), later known as International Amusement Devices (now defunct). Their deep, cushioned seating, heavy weight, generous chrome trim, and other Art Deco touches (including headlights on some models) make them a favorite of coaster connoisseurs, and they provide a solid, comfortable ride.

Builders of steel coasters—Arrow, Schwarzkopf, Bollinger & Mabillard among them—generally build their

Over the years, the style of coaster cars and trains seem to have varied as much as that of the automobile. Some coaster vehicles are custom built by private contractors; others are fabricated by manufacturers specializing in coaster and amusement ride construction. In a few instances, some parks built their coaster trains in-house. (Chicago's Riverview Park did this through its subsidiary, Riverview Construction Company.) Often it's easy to identify a coaster train's manufacturer just by looking at its design.

Philadelphia Toboggan Coasters (formerly Philadelphia Toboggan Company) is one of today's most productive coaster train manufacturers, and PTC's wood-track coaster vehicles are the Chevrolets of coaster vehicles. PTC, which built coasters itself until the 1970s, now concentrates primarily on supplying parks and ride designers with trains and replacement parts for its own wooden coaster vehicles, along with braking and queue gate systems (remotely controlled locking gates in the station area that keep queues of guests safely away from the track until the train is ready for boarding).

own rolling stock since each of those manufacturer's coasters are so specialized in terms of track design. Wood-track coasters generally are more standardized and can accept the trains of more than one manufacturer.

Recently, a number of international wood-track coaster–train builders have emerged, but perhaps the most attractive new entry is America's own Great Coasters International, which in 1999 began offering its own version of the single seat (two riders per car) trailered coaster train. Inspired by the magnificent rolling stock developed by Fred Church for his *Bob*s twisters during the first golden age of roller coasters, GCI's Michael Boodley and his team of engineers followed suit. With their own rides becoming more twisted and intense, they needed a train with a very short wheelbase that would enable it to effectively handle the new convoluted track layouts. These retro-inspired, though thoroughly modern trains (chapter 5) perform as marvelously as their golden-age counterparts, proving the age-old adage, "what's past is prologue."

PTC WITH A DETROIT TOUCH

The trains of Philadelphia Toboggan Company can be found on more wood coasters than those of any other manufacturer. For nearly a century, PTC has been providing rolling stock for coasters. Overall, PTC's train design and construction has remained remarkably unchanged through the years, with some interesting twists, such as these automobile-nose-styled trains on the *Comet* at Forest Park Highlands in St. Louis. The scene dates from circa 1950. *PTC*

CLASSIC PRE-RENAISSANCE PTC

Simple and utilitarian is the look of this PTC on the *Jackrabbit* at Wildwood, New Jersey, in 1973. This was the look of many PTC trains manufactured after World War II and before the 1970s. The hallmark of PTC trains of this era was the sloped front end with the curved top. As the twentieth century ended, only *Roller Coaster* at Joyland Park in Wichita, Kansas, was operating its original PTC trains, which were of this lineage. *Tom Halterman*

NAD CENTURY FLYERS

Long a favorite of dedicated coaster fans are the solid trains manufactured by National Amusement Device. Very Art Deco, these heavy-duty trains featured deep cushioned seating and aluminum and wood construction with stainless-steel sheathing. Dubbed "Century Flyers" (note the Century Flyer nose emblem on this *Big Dipper* train at Camden Park, Huntington, West Virginia, in 1991), these trains often featured headlights, which some parks actually operated. NAD trains can still be found on several North American coasters. *Mike Schafer*

NATURE OF THE RIDE

Roller coasters, especially wooden ones, tend to have their own unique personalities—it's all a part of the nature of the ride. A longtime highly regarded ride, the *Coaster* (now known as the *Thunderhawk*) at Dorney Park, Allentown, Pennsylvania, has an interesting combination of elements that make it stand out from other coasters: a curving first drop; a low-level "speed bump" between the first drop and following major hill; and a twisting knot of trackage—shown here in 1980—at the outer end of the ride that slams riders against the sides of the car or their seat partners. The trains return home from this wooden bowtie section via a series of rabbit-hop hills. *Mike Schafer*

continued from page 79

(usually four wheelsets to a car). With an articulated train, adjacent cars share "trucks" or "bogies" (wheel assemblies), thereby reducing the overall weight of the train and allowing for smoother flow over the course. Most steel-track coaster trains are of this design. With a trailer-type articulated train, the forward end of each car is wheelless and is supported by the wheeled back end of the preceding car. Trailered trains have very flexible wheelbases and therefore are ideal on wooden coasters that have particularly gnarled track layouts.

The model of train chosen for any given coaster depends on the type of ride itself, the maximum number of patrons the park wishes to handle efficiently, and construction budgets. Some parks will adjust train size to meet anticipated customer demand. After King's Island (Cincinnati) opened its *Beast* roller coaster in 1979, the wild coaster's popularity required the park to add a car to each of the ride's trains.

The Nature of the Ride

A spin aboard a good wooden coaster will include instances when riders may feel as if their train has left the track—especially at the crests of low-lying hills

where speed is greatest. But rest assured the upstop wheels will prevent cars from becoming airborne. The same goes for the feeling that your rocketing train might hurtle off the track as it careens around a tight turn. The horizontal guide wheels and, again, the upstop wheels inhibit this action and keep the train safely on course, though you might end up a bit chummier with your seat mate.

The above-mentioned out-of-seat incidents are something many coaster enthusiasts actually look for in what they consider a brilliant roller coaster. That feeling of the tractor wheels momentarily lifting off the rails and riders' bodies floating during zero- or negative-gravity moments is referred to in enthusiast circles as "airtime." It is a cherished sensation for the avid thrillseeker, as is the feeling of being pinned to the side of the car when the train roars through a reckless turn or a wicked transition in the track. These lateral Gs are also an ingredient many fans look for in their favorite rides.

Most coaster designers, on the other hand, strive to limit and control these seemingly out-of-control movements. They must keep in mind that the wilder the ride, the more punishing the action on the trains and structure, which will require more maintenance. A good designer will knowingly calculate just the right amount of airtime and lateral Gs into a ride to produce the expected thrill while keeping tolerances within safe and comfortable limits.

Generally, wooden coasters offer a more rambunctious ride than their steel equivalents. Because of their very nature, they are loud, rattling, turbulent adventures, with some a bit more uninhibited than others. Compared to the unforgiving character of a steel coaster, woodies may look rather fragile. In reality, the wooden framework is far more formidable than its appearance suggests. When it came time to level the seemingly rickety *Rocket* at Ocean View Park, Norfolk, Virginia, after its use in the film *The Death of Ocean View Park*, demolition crews gave up trying to pull and push it down with bulldozers and instead resorted to dynamite and chainsaws!

A wooden coaster's seemingly delicate visage is just part of its mystique—that all-important illusion of danger. The fact that portions of the structure will

visibly sway and shake when the heavy trains thunder past is a factor intentionally built into the ride. The structure must remain flexible to absorb the forces generated by the combined weight of trains and passengers. This wave-like "give" acts as a natural shock absorber, flowing with the dynamics created by the screeching cars and then springing back when the train has moved on. For whatever reason, the accompanying audible creaking and groaning of the superstructure can instill absolute terror in potential riders. Such is the charm of a woodie.

Though steel coasters are generally smoother because of their "soft" wheels, they, too, have their severe moments. For example, the positive G forces encountered during loops or tight spirals can be as punishing to some riders as the shake, rattle, and roll produced by wooden coasters. Furthermore, some steel coasters are more brutal due to poorly designed track transitions and/or the placement of over-the-shoulder passenger restraint systems—almost universally used by coasters with inversions.

The Best Seat in the House

Ask any two coaster enthusiasts which ride is their favorite, or where on the train they like to sit, and you'll end up opening a virtual Pandora's box of

BEST SEAT IN THE HOUSE?

Another unending debate among coaster connoisseurs is whether the front or back seat is best. The front seat can offer spectacular views like this aboard the restored *Giant Dipper* at Belmont Park in San Diego, California. A front seat on this cherished ride gives riders this view of the twisted first plunge off the lift hill. *Terry Lind*

WILDCAT, DAYTON, OHIO

A bonafied legend, the *Wildcat* at Lakeside Park in Dayton, Ohio, featured a swooping drop off the lift hill (upper left in photo; the drop is partially obscured by trees in this aerial view from circa 1950) as well as other hills. Note the ride's several tunnels, some short, some long (the entire approach to the lift hill was enclosed). Park-goers used to gather at trackside after dark to watch the trains spray sparks as they hurtled around the ride's vicious turns. For a diagram of the ride's convoluted track layout, see the facing page.
Marvin Christian

rhetoric and debate. This is only natural, since every person has individual tastes and preferences. That's why so-called "top ten" lists of favorite coasters can vary so greatly (and, no, biggest *isn't* always best).

Still, there are certain reasons to choose one particular seat over another, since the resulting experiences can differ quite dramatically. Basically, the rear seats of the train, especially those in the last car, offer a wilder ride, due to the fact that they are being pulled over the hills by the weight of the forward cars. Depending on your point of view, this whip-like action can make for a harrowing or euphoric ride. This is especially true in coasters with long trains on steep hills, because much of the downhill is experienced at a faster rate of speed.

On the other hand, the benefits of sitting up front score major points. If you make it into the front seat, the view will be outstanding, guaranteed. After chain release, the front cars hang over the first drop,

waiting for the rest of the train to crest the hill. Another advantage of sampling the forward seats is that airtime at the tops of hills, particularly low-speed bumps, can be more extreme. On some rides famous for their low-G moments, front-seat riders can expect to do quite a bit of floating.

If you're still not sure, gravitate toward the center of the train, where the ride is usually the smoothest. When you get a feel for the coaster and you talk yourself back on, graduate to the first and last seats.

Creating the Madness

Designing roller coasters is an exclusive and highly specialized profession. Just as the rides themselves have evolved over the years, so have the techniques employed to create them.

In the early years, some designers were trained in the building methods of the day. Others were simply gifted visionaries who learned from experience,

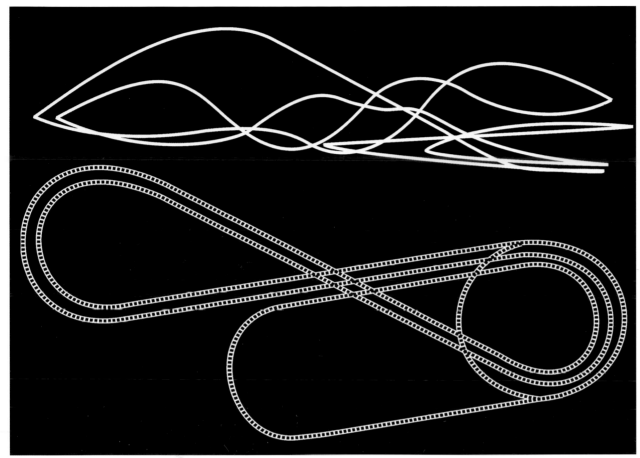

working alongside those already adept at erecting coasters. They eventually took that accumulated knowledge and hands-on education to execute their own rides. It was in that period that coaster plans were drawn by hand on vellum and blueprints, numbered with the intended measurements, and then handed over to the construction team who would render into reality what the designer had envisioned.

Most of the time the completed rides performed quite well, while there were some that had to be adjusted and reworked in the field before they could take on their first passengers. Back then, coaster designers did not have the luxury of computers or calculators but instead had to rely on their experience, gut instinct, and construction skills.

Though the process happens quite differently today, it pretty much achieves the same desired result. Blueprints were eventually replaced by building from specifications. Drawings are still used to a degree, but they are mainly assembled within the virtual reality of super-fast computers. Advanced structural and mechanical engineering and manufacturing techniques bring the project to life at the site.

As chapter 6 explains, hi-resolution computer-generated animation and three-dimensional capabilities are being utilized more often to give the designer and the client a rather convincing and wholly realistic visual idea of what they can expect in their new coaster.

Regardless of how much education engineers have under their belts, they must also be artists. Creative vision and imagination are necessary to bring about the rides they intend to construct. They must also be aware of human nature and just what the body can endure. But above all else, they should possess an unwavering passion for their work. When a designer obviously enjoys what he does, the result of that love and dedication burns brightly in the finished product.

4

Postwar Coastering

1945–1972: A Lull Before the Storm

THE *THUNDERBOLT*(S)

Luck and patience, not trick photography, resulted in this late-evening scene of a thunderstorm sweeping in over Kennywood Park and its star attraction, the *Thunderbolt* coaster. The scene is symbolic of the tumultuous period for parks and their roller coasters that followed World War II and the coaster revival that began early in the 1970s. The *Thunderbolt* was unveiled in 1968 after the Pittsburgh-area park performed a major overhaul on its old *Pippin* coaster. It was a silver lining to an often cloudy era. *Mike Schafer*

The Depression had begun to ebb by 1939, and as conditions improved, the surviving parks placed orders for new rides. The big-band era was in full swing near the end of the decade, and many parks had their dancing pavilions and other buildings retrofitted with the new Art Deco style of architecture. Great films like the Wizard of Oz and Gone With the Wind inspired audiences, world's fairs in New York, Chicago, and San Francisco gave the planet hope, and it seemed the future had brightened considerably. But on the Depression's heels was World War II.

ENTERTAINING THE TROOPS

Well guarded by an platoon of servicemen, a woman passenger has the best seat in the house on the *Flying Turns* at Euclid Beach, Cleveland. Happy faces on all the riders hide the terrible pall of World War II hanging over America. Amusement parks and their coasters helped divert attention from the horrors of battle. *The Cleveland Plain Dealer*

LET THE GOOD TIMES ROLL

With the war over, Americans resumed their penchant for play. In this 1946 tableau of postwar exuberance, Clevelanders crowd the boarding platforms and trains of the *Thriller* at Euclid Beach. *The Cleveland Plain Dealer*

The United States' entrance into the war in December 1941 had a major impact on American life. Gas rationing, blackouts, and the draft became the norm. Amusement parks that could afford to buy new attractions were forced to purchase used rides from various sources as many ride companies had changed their manufacturing format to produce products necessary for the war effort. As a result, materials for upkeep were difficult to find. Once again, ingenious maintenance crews had to make do with what they had to keep the parks open and operating as the war raged on. Regardless, parks had their own role in the war effort, serving as a diversion for home-bound folks who otherwise had to face the daily reports of the ongoing horror overseas. At a time when air-raid drills were a common occurrence, park management was determined to maintain a sense of optimism and give the people a safe, affordable place to play while their world was on shaky ground.

Patriotism was readily visible at the nation's amusement parks. Members of the armed forces in full uniform frequented parks, enjoying rides and attractions—sometimes complements of park management. Since rubber and gasoline were high on the list of wartime rations, auto traffic plummeted and so did park attendance except where one could still reach parks via public transit.

The postwar euphoria that swept through America following Armistice Day in 1945 would produce effects so far-reaching that they are still being felt—chief among them the great baby boom which would last well into the 1960s. The crescendo for change rapidly increased beginning about 1947, by which time members of the armed forces had returned to

THE *COMET*, HERSHEY, PENNSYLVANIA

One of the first "baby boomer" coasters to open following World War II was the *Comet* at Hershey Amusement Park—in the back yard of famed chocolate producer Hershey—near Harrisburg. This Schmeck-designed PTC ride debuted in 1946, and it's been a park favorite ever since. The T-shaped track layout provides numerous classic hills traversed at a fast pace. *Otto P. Dobnick*

CRYSTAL BEACH COMET

Another *Comet* landed on earth right after the war when Crystal Beach, on the Ontario shore of Lake Erie near Buffalo, New York, unveiled its newest coaster. Another Schmeck/PTC classic, this *Comet* became revered for its high turnarounds and low intermediate hills—a combination that makes for great "air time." Since this 1984 photo, the *Comet* has been moved some 270 miles east to Lake George, New York. *Mike Schafer*

U.S. soil and settled down to raise families and get back to business—which meant launching new endeavors or improving existing ones. For amusement parks, this was, in part good news. Existing infrastructure could now be repaired, especially wooden roller coasters, many of which were overhauled and cosmetically improved. New buildings and rides were erected. In 1945, for example, Geauga Lake (now Six Flags Ohio) near Cleveland, Ohio, renovated its superb 1926 woodie, the *Big Dipper*. In 1946 a classic which still reigns supreme

opened at Hershey Amusement Park (now Hersheypark), Hershey, Pennsylvania: the *Comet*. Built by PTC. This 82-foot-high favorite was typical of a Schmeck-designed coaster with its excellent drops, speed humps, and fast pacing.

Three more Schmeck coasters of note followed the *Comet* in 1947, 1948, and 1949. At Playland Park in San Antonio, Texas, Schmeck's *Rocket* roller coaster opened in 1947. With a lift hill of less than 80 feet and a figure-8 track plan, the rollicking *Rocket* thrived more than a quarter of a century in relative obscurity thrilling patrons deep in the heart of Texas. The *Rocket* closed in the 1970s, and then through an interesting twist of fate rose to stardom in the late 1980s deep in the heart of Pennsylvania as the *Phoenix* (chapter 5).

The Schmeck winner from 1948 was the new *Comet* at Crystal Beach, Ontario. Though intended as a more mild-mannered replacement for Crystal Beach's notorious Traver *Cyclone*, the new *Comet* had nothing to apologize for. The nearly 100-foot tall ride, which used steel structural components from the *Cyclone*, featured high turnarounds and low "speed bump" hills to hurtle trains along its 4,000-foot-plus course. The *Comet* became one of the star "baby boomer" coasters of the postwar period, and remains so to this day. Like the Playland *Rocket*, the *Comet* endured a hiatus before reopening in Lake George, New York, in 1994.

Schmeck/PTC closed out the 1940s with the opening of *Roller Coaster* at Joyland Park, Wichita, Kansas, in 1949. Very much a family-oriented ride, this 80-foot-high coaster still performs admirably for patrons at this off-the-beaten-path park and was still using its original PTC trains as of 2000.

The Art Deco influence was still apparent in park décor although a new postwar "modern" influence was emerging. A decade and half of depression and war had been tough. Gone were many of the local "neighborhood" parks, but the survivors, mostly bigger parks—among them the Coney Island parks, Cleveland's Euclid Beach, Pittsburgh's Kennywood, Chicago's Riverview, Denver's Lakeside, and Los Angeles' Long Beach and Venice piers—looked to the future . . . and some unexpected challenges

The 1950s: Competition and Other Problems

Postwar prosperity invigorated the country, but it was relatively short-lived for amusement parks. The arrival of the 1950s found America in a state of flux. Tastes were changing, and a relaxed social attitude became apparent. Technology, meanwhile, was advancing exponentially: The invention of something called television brought a new, high-tech threat for amusement parks.

Television advocates preached the virtues of in-home entertainment and disdained amusement institutions and motion-picture theaters, proclaiming that the amusement park (and therefore its roller coasters) had served their purpose and the time to move on to more modern diversions had arrived. The threat was very real, but thankfully not all parks adhered to this notion.

Few new coasters were built during the 1950s. PTC constructed several "kiddie" or "junior" coasters (sidebar) catering to young baby boomers that had swelled America's postwar population, and otherwise survived by rehabbing or rebuilding existing coasters. PTC was still alive, but its only major rides during this decade were the *Comet* at Fontaine Ferry Park in Louisville, Kentucky, in 1951 and the *Mighty Lightnin'* at Rocky Glen Park between Scranton and Wilkes-Barre, Pennsylvania, in 1958. Also in 1958, Camden Park near Huntington, West Virginia, unveiled its modest-size but lots-of-fun *Big Dipper* coaster, built by National Amusement Device. Beyond that, the pickings were slim.

Image was another threat to parks and their coasters during the 1950s and 1960s. The rebelliousness of American youth in the postwar years often

CYCLONE, PALISADES PARK, NEW JERSEY

Famed Palisades Park at Fort Lee, New Jersey, overlooking the Hudson River and Manhattan Island, was one of a legion of parks that would survive the postwar era, only to succumb to urban redevelopment just as the coaster renaissance got under way in the early 1970s. This 1950s view shows the park's celebrated *Cyclone*. *Chuck Davis*

Kiddie and Junior Coasters

With a new crop of babies on the rise after World War II, parks began looking for coaster rides that kids could teeth on. Most regulation-size coasters had age and/or height restrictions that precluded folks under 8 or so from riding. Not fair!

Shortly after the close of the war, Herbert Schmeck and the Philadelphia Toboggan Company developed a semi-standardized, scaled-down, wood-track coaster—complete with elfin PTC-style coaster trains (with flanged wheels, however)—that could be ridden by youngsters and even by toddlers with their parents. Generally, these kiddie coasters had lift hills about 25 feet tall, with a 16-foot drop; track layout employed a figure-8 design. From these kiddie versions evolved the "junior" coasters, with lift hills around 45 feet tall and a longer run, though with the same figure-8 track arrangement. John Allen picked up where Schmeck left off and designed numerous PTC kiddie and junior coasters, several of which still operate.

Other companies featured their own versions of these pint-size coasters. The Herschel Company's *Little Dipper* line of all-steel coasters (with flat L-girder track, not tubular) also became popular at kiddie parks (or in the children's section of a big park) while National Amusement Device offered a line of wood-track junior coasters, the last of which—the *Lil' Dipper*—operates at Camden Park near Huntington, West Virginia. Portable kiddie and junior coasters also became the rage for traveling carnivals in the 1950s. Some contemporary coaster builders offer kiddie coasters in their product line.

The idea for a kid-friendly coaster was not really a postwar product. In 1928, the L. A. Thompson Company (of La Marcus Thompson fame) built its last coaster, the *Kiddie Coaster*, which circles the kiddieland section of Playland Park at Rye, New York. This rare and unusual ride, which features mini NAD rolling stock, still operates.

SEA DRAGON, WYANDOT LAKE, COLUMBUS, OHIO
The woodie residing at the Wyandot Lake is a pristine example of a PTC junior coaster. Of the versions erected in 1956, this is the only remaining example of John Allen's very first design. Despite the *Jet Flyer* name on the train, the park refers to its coaster as the *Sea Dragon*. Otto P. Dobnick

KIDDIE COASTER, PLAYLAND PARK, RYE, NEW YORK
This Munchkin-size ride is one of the most unusual wood-track coasters around. The *Kiddie Coaster* was the last coaster built by the once-famed L. A. Thompson Company. It's three-car trailered trains by National Amusement Device circle the kids' section of Playland on wood structurework. Unfortunately, you have to be a kid to ride this historic gem. *Otto P. Dobnick.*

manifested itself at traditional amusement parks, and the public came to view parks as hangouts for hooligans and other miscreants. Part of the problem was that many traditional amusement parks were wide open. Folks could wander in and out at will with no or minimal charge for admission; payment was made only for ride tickets. (At Riverview Park in Chicago, admission to the park was as little as nickel on some days, even in the 1960s.) Thus, city-based parks in particular often became an ad hoc babysitter for neighborhood kids on warm summer days and were subject to the unfortunate effects of what happens with crowds of unsupervised youth. A talented and pioneering dreamer in Southern California was about to change that.

Walt Disney and the Theme Park Concept

Just as traditional amusement parks and surviving trolley parks seemed to be entering their twilight years—some struggling simply to survive the new television era—a very interesting situation was developing in Southern California. Walter Elias Disney was keenly aware of the rapid demise of amusement parks around the country. By the same token, he was dismayed at the gaudy carnival atmosphere that pervaded many pleasure parks of that era. His recalls of the halcyon days of the amusement places he had visited as a boy spurred him into action. The time had arrived, he decided, to transform into reality a dream he had been considering for a long time.

Already made wealthy by the success of his Mickey Mouse character, Walt Disney had "toys" at his disposal that most kids could only dream about, chief among them a miniature live-steam railroad—large enough to ride—in his huge back yard. Several sources suggest that this railroad was the initial spark that ignited the creative firestorm that would eventually yield Disneyland. Walt had long thought it would be wonderful to have a fully functioning pleasure railroad encircling a new type of amusement park.

With his animation and film studios doing a brisk business, he sought the help of his artists and animators to develop the concept he had envisioned. Disney wished to create a self-contained environment that

could transport guests away from the real world to a place where fantasy and fun reigned supreme, a wonderland where families could go together and feel completely safe and protected. He imagined the rides

"The biggest new entertainment event of the year." - LIFE

and attractions to be unlike anything ever devised. His rides would be housed within elaborate movie film–like sets with well-orchestrated story lines. Like one of his movies, every aspect of this new concept would be planned and executed in minute detail.

Though few people understood his vision or even believed the public would pay to visit such a place, Disney had unwavering faith in his idea. And, as in his other creative endeavors, his enthusiasm was infectious. With the assistance of his studio staff, he set into motion a grand scheme that would eventually become the "Happiest Place on Earth."

Constructed in Anaheim, California, this magnificent new "theme park" opened its gates in 1955, and the amusement industry hasn't been the same since. Though a few other parks claim to have originated the theme-park idea prior to Disney, it was Disneyland that defined and perfected the concept, setting the standard for virtually all theme parks which followed.

THIS IS CINERAMA

Early in the 1950s, a new cinema sensation helped awaken coaster awareness. Dubbed "Cinerama," this new movie-house scheme utilized a three-camera projection system and a huge surround-the-audience screen. A pioneer to today's IMAX movie experience, Cinerama drew the audience right into the movie, which made the first production, *This Is Cinerama*, a natural for a front-seat coaster ride segment. Postcards of the era such as this distributed by the Cinerama company used an artist's rendering to overstate the coaster sequence, which in reality was filmed aboard the *Atom Smasher* coaster at Rockaway's Playland near New York City. *Scott Rutherford collection*

What did this have to do with the roller coaster? Nothing. . . and then everything. Roller coasters initially were non-existent on Disney's roster of necessary attractions. He felt the rattling wooden contraptions had no place in his futuristic and fanciful park. Although the public had readily embraced Disney's new theme-park concept and Disneyland's interesting new rides, there was still a fundamental desire for the unique type of physical thrills that coaster rides provided. This is why new parks that embraced the theme-park concept *and* coasters would do so well in the coming years.

The Modern Steel Roller Coaster is Born

Disney finally decided to give the roller coaster another chance, but of course not in the traditional manner of soaring wooden bents and roaring coaster trains. Rather, he would disguise his coaster with a theme of some type. During a vacation in Switzerland, he reportedly became fascinated with the idea of a bobsled run. Originally, he instructed his designers to consider the idea of transforming the compact, steel-track *Wild Mouse* coasters that had been popularized in the mid-1950s (sidebar) into an attraction that would simulate a bobsled run down the side of a scaled-down version of the Matterhorn. Of course, the ride had to conform to Disney's lofty standards of excellence, and when the Disney staff realized it simply could not make a coaster running on flat steel rails smooth and enjoyable enough to live up to Disney's expectations, they had to consider another design approach.

Disney called on industry pioneers Carl Bacon and Ed Morgan of Arrow Development, a small manufacturing firm based in Northern California. Arrow had already built several well-received ride systems for Disneyland, so Walt pitched the bobsled/Matterhorn idea to Bacon and Morgan. He told them to come up with a brand-new steel-coaster concept—fast.

MATTERHORN BOBSLEDS

Opened in 1959, this was the first Disney roller coaster and the one which started the steel roller coaster revolution. Arrow Development's (now Arrow Dynamics) use of tubular steel rails and a soft compound for the wheels set the precedent for virtually every steel coaster that would follow. Unknown to the casual observer, the *Matterhorn* is in reality two separate though intertwined coaster systems. Inside the Matterhorn mountain replica which shrouds most of the coasters, riders enjoy a chilly encounter with the abominable snowman. Afterward they are treated to a snappy bobsled tour of the mountain and a watery splashdown finale. *Walt Disney Productions*

Instead of a midway simply lined with rides and games of chance, Disneyland was comprised of a central Main Street, which lead to a whimsical and highly detailed interpretation of Sleeping Beauty's castle. This elegant structure was the center or hub of the park. And from this hub, other avenues branched out and led to individually themed lands such as Tomorrowland, Fantasyland, Frontierland, and Adventureland. Key to the whole thing was the controlled access and an admission price that kept rif-raff at bay.

Despite some early snafus, Disney's "imagineers" created escapism on a gargantuan scale, turning Disneyland into a showcase of the Disney product line and an amusement park like no other on Earth. The new venture was squeaky clean and as close to perfect as humanly possible. With his theme-park concept, Disney guided the amusement industry in a brand-new direction and gave this once-popular form of outdoor entertainment a much needed boost.

Rodents Gone Berserk

Although the steel-track roller coaster did not truly come of age until the 1970s, along about mid century there emerged a series of steel-track coasters that earned a place in the world of coasters. In fact, the *Wild Mouse* and its kin were making a comeback at the close of the twentieth century.

Although a European ride manufacture claims to have built the first *Wild Mouse* in 1954, the ride also appeared in the U.S. around the same time. Regardless, the basic premise of the *Wild Mouse* was simple—but effective: Several small, two-passengers cars (often shaped like little cartoon rodents) travel on a narrow track whose rails are comprised of steel L-girder rails; the track is shaped into a compact collection of tight hairpin turns and abrupt drops. The ride's support structure was usually made of a seemingly delicate maze of thin wooden (later, steel) supports.

From the ground, the *Wild Mouse* was frightening because of its fragile appearance. From a rider's viewpoint, it was scary for the same reason, but also because the vehicles sat rather high above the track and sported an extremely short wheelbase that was recessed toward the center of the car. This precarious arrangement made the nose of the car protrude over the edge of the track on curves, thereby giving the unnerving illusion that the speeding vehicles were actually going to soar out into midair as they careened about the ride. Urban legends abound of this actually happening, but documented proof of such incidents has not surfaced as of this writing.

Though Ben Schiff is often credited as the actual inventor of the 1950s *Wild Mouse* rides, other designers of the period built similar versions with like names: *Mad Mouse*, *Wild Chipmunk*, *Monster Mouse*. Examples of these are still in operation today. Some *Wild Mouse*es, including that which was the centerpiece of the amusement area of the 1960 Seattle World's Fair, were even built with a laminated wood track much like their larger full-size roller coaster cousins. These wood-track *Wild Mouse*es are considered to be among the most popular in *Mouse*-connoisseur circles, and two are still operating in England. The *Wild Mouse* at Blackpool Pleasure Beach, built in-house, is undoubtedly one of the most outrageous such rides ever built. (A word of advice: hang on!) Several modified manifestations of the *Mouse* rides produced by Fred Miler and the Miler Coaster Company during this period are still popular at the parks they inhabit today.

Virtually every modern steel coaster manufacturer now offers an updated version of the *Wild Mouse*, some of which even feature spinning cars.

MAD MOUSE

When the first *Wild Mouse* rides came on line in the 1950s, they became an overnight sensation, spawning not only more *Wild Mouse* rides but *Wild Mouse* wannabes, including a ride known as the *Mad Mouse*. Slightly less elaborate than a true *Wild Mouse*, the *Mad Mouse*—this installation is shown in 1986 at the now-closed Enchanted Forest near Chesterton, Indiana—still followed the premise of its bigger cousin: zig-zag track with impossibly sharp turns and sudden drops. *Otto P. Dobnick*

After much brainstorming and field testing at its fabrication plant, Arrow hit upon a unique track system that would ultimately change the face of the amusement industry forever. Morgan and Bacon knew that bending angle iron into a smooth track was impracticable, so they steered clear of the typical flat rails used on the *Wild Mouse* rides and instead developed a track comprised of two hollow metal tubes to serve as the ride's running rails.

Among the several conditions Disney insisted upon was that the ride be quiet and comfortable as well as completely safe. In other words, make it as different as possible from a *Wild Mouse*. To meet Disney's goals, Arrow finally developed the ingenious concept of using a steel wheel coated with polyurethane produced by DuPont in place of a hard steel wheel. Polyurethane had advantages over the other possible wheel coatings considered, such as rubber and nylon: It produced the least amount of loss to friction and maintained its structural integrity during temperature fluctuations and under varying weight loads.

Another manner in which Arrow's ride differed

SALTAIR

Built on a huge fill on the Great Salt Lake west of Salt Lake City, Utah, Saltair amusement park was another trolley park, having been built and operated by the Salt Lake, Garfield & Western Railway interurban line. The park's final coaster was known as the *Giant Racer* and is partially visible in this view taken on September 6, 1957, after the park had closed for the season. *John Dziobko*

MIGHTY LIGHTNIN'

One of only two major coasters built by PTC during the 1950s, the *Mighty Lightnin'* (at different times also known as the *Comet* or *Jet Star*) was a typical John Allen design. The park it called home, Rocky Glen, and later Ghost Town in the Glen, featured several wooden coasters throughout its long history. Its final woodie closed with the park in 1987 and sat dormant until its demolition in 1994. A virtual copy of the ride can be found at Strickler's Grove, Ross, Ohio. *Mike Schafer*

from the *Wild Mouse* was evident in the coaster vehicles. Arrow lowered the car's center of gravity by positioning the car almost between the rails instead of having it teeter and rock precariously above them. This made the vehicle much more stable, thereby meeting the all-important safety factor Disney required in his attractions.

The result of Arrow's enormous amount of research and development was Disneyland's famous *Matterhorn Bobsleds*. This historically important ride opened to the public in 1959 and was an instant success. Though the ride has aged and gone through several rehabs, it is still one of the most popular attractions at Disneyland. The public knew it all along: there's nothing like roller coaster.

Like Disneyland itself, Arrow's groundbreaking technology revolutionized the amusement industry overnight. With its complex dual-track design and multiple low-slung bobsleds swirling down, through, and around a 147-foot-tall replica of the famous Swiss mountain peak, the *Matterhorn* gave Disney-

continued on page 100

LA MONTANA RUSA, MEXICO CITY

One of the most significant postwar/pre-renaissance coasters, *La Montana Rusa* is the centerpiece of La Feria in Mexico City's Chapultepec Park. This 110-foot tall, 4,000-foot long thriller is considered NAD's crowning achievement and is one of only three existing racing coasters with a continuous (interconnected) track arrangement. This 1989 photo depicts the imposing ride before a modernization program (which included track modifications) removed some of this legend's savage and wonderfully terrifying negative-G forces. *Scott Rutherford*

BIG DIPPER, CAMDEN PARK, HUNTINGTON, WEST VIRGINIA

Though not a large ride, the 1958-built *Big Dipper* is historically important for several reasons. Currently it is West Virginia's only major wooden coaster and was one of the few woodies built during the postwar industry slump. The *Dipper* features NAD Century Flyer rolling stock and remains a classic ride in a great park. *Terry Lind*

Mister Twister and a Thunderbolt

The period following World War II and before the start of the roller coaster renaissance in 1972 certainly had its desolate moments for the amusement industry. The country itself seemed to be experiencing its own roller coaster ride with valleys of bad times (the Kennedy assassination of 1963; the Vietnam War) and good (the carefree 1950s; the Beatles; the lunar landing of 1969).

During this quarter century period, a few shining stars shone on coasterdom's darkened landscape. Here are two notable rides, built during the industry's rocky days, which were instrumental in keeping alive the art of wooden–roller coaster design.

Mister Twister, Elitch Gardens, Denver

Coaster designer John Allen will be most remembered for his wildest creation: the outstanding *Mister Twister* (later simply known as *Twister*) at Denver's original Elitch Gardens. The ride, as unveiled in 1964 was a bomb. The lift hill immediately dropped trains into a slow-paced double helix (interlaced with the *Wildcat* coaster) followed by a hum-drum run back to the station. Perturbed by lackluster reviews, Allen launched an investigation and reportedly found an error on the blueprints that had resulted in the first hill being angled at 42.5 degrees rather than the intended 45 degrees—which illustrates just how drastic a ride's performance can be effected by a seemingly minor deviations.

But Allen went beyond merely correcting the slope problem. Apparently urged by park management to rethink the entire ride, Allen added a higher lift hill and two deep plunges which lead into the old double helix—at breakneck speed. A harrowing drop turn through a hidden tunnel followed the helix, and the ride concluded with a rabbit-hop trip through the trestlework back to the station, with a final hump lifting passengers from their seats as the train screamed back into the station. Allen had created a world-class thriller that would gain cult status during the renaissance.

ELITCH GARDENS' *TWISTER*
Twister was a tangle of track, part of which included the camelback hills of *Twister*'s sister, the *Wildcat*. *Mike Schafer*

THUNDERBOLT

Intertwine new (left) and old (above) coaster trackage and what do you get? Kennywood's all-time favorite coaster, the *Thunderbolt*. *Mike Schafer*

Unveiled in 1965, the new *Mister Twister* was a barely restrained thriller unlike anything traditionalist John Allen had ever created. Ironically, he was not fond of the ride, but that had no effect on its popularity. *Twister* remained a beloved favorite of riders everywhere right up to its final operating day in 1994, when Elitch Gardens began the move to a larger location, abandoning its crown jewel and the *Wildcat*. Relocated to downtown Denver, the new Elitch Gardens opened with a new coaster called *Twister II* in 1995, a wild ride in its own right that mimics its world-class predecessor.

Twister stood silent until 1999 when this proud example of roller coaster genius was unceremoniously leveled—but not without inspiring new rides. Aside from cousin *Twister II*, Knoebel's Grove Park in Pennsylvania unveiled its *Twister* in mid-summer 1999. Based on the plans of the Elitch *Twister*, the Knoebel's modified version closely invokes the sensational thrill of the original.

Thunderbolt, Kennywood Park, West Mifflin, Pennsylvania

While other parks were closing in record numbers, Kennywood enjoyed success in the 1960s. Management had been adding a new ride each season for several years and wanted to maintain that momentum by rebuilding one of its early wooden coasters. The *Jack Rabbit* was a contender, but eventually park management zeroed in on John Miller's 1923-built *Pippin*. Kennywood's own Andy Vettel, of the famed Vettel coaster–building clan, would oversee the job. The reworking of the *Pippin* was quietly initiated during the winter of 1967 and completed for the 1968 operating season.

Vettel kept the *Pippin*'s impressive ravine section intact and added a high section of track on the flat area where the *Pippin*'s station had been located. When a swirling new collection of undulating hills and turns was integrated into the old ravine section, the *Thunderbolt*—and a new coaster legend—was born. Thanks to the ingenious new track layout, Kennywood had a coaster whose drops got larger as the ride went on!

The new *Thunderbolt* used magnificent four-car Century Flyers that had been purchased from National Amusement Device for *Pippin* service. The trains began their circuit with a plunge out of the station into the hidden "back 40" *Pippin* portion of the ride nested in a deep ravine. A tunnel, a second drop, and a long chain lift out of the valley took the silver trains up to the new section looming on a bluff over the Monongahela River. After completing the rollicking new segments of the ride, riders were unexpectedly flung back into the ravine on old *Pippin* trackage, not once, but twice. The *Thunderbolt*'s final 90-foot drop was and is the ride's biggest. Such an unpredictable layout and breathtaking finale are what earned the *Thunderbolt* a loyal following that grows in force with each passing season. Today, a ride on the *Thunderbolt* is a rite of passage for Pittsburghers as well as any up-and-coming coaster enthusiast.

Kennywood is one of the world's finest traditional amusement parks. And as long as it is home to classic wooden roller coasters like the *Thunderbolt*, its future is ensured.

continued from page 97

land its first real thrill ride. This new breed of roller coaster helped revitalize roller coaster manufacturing and initiated a wave of new and exciting rides that continues to this day.

Ups and Downs of the 1960s

That turbulent period between the late 1950s and the end of the 1960s was significant for a number of reasons. A major recession in 1958 found American citizens leaving behind an age of innocence and entering a time of rebellion and unrest—a situation especially evident in the inner cities. The tight-knit communities located in the thriving metropoli were being abandoned as urban dwellers sought to leave

BLUE STREAK, RIVERVIEW PARK, CHICAGO

Chicago's famed Riverview Park was home to several Miller & Baker coasters over the years. Standing at the north end of the park was the *Blue Streak*, shown in the late 1940s with its unusual shrouded trains and double-dip first drop over the station. In 1960, this ride received a major makeover when it was rebuilt as the *Fireball* (right). *Mike Schafer collection*

FIREBALL, RIVERVIEW PARK

The photo at right was taken on August 9, 1960, at virtually the same location and angle as the color view above of the *Blue Streak*. Gone is the *Blue Streak*'s double-dipping first drop and in its place a harrowing plunge that tunnels completely under the new station—which itself has been given a major face lift with campy "fireball" theming; note the fireball head atop the ride's ticket booth at center right in the photo. Several coaster rides throughout the U.S. were modified during the postwar era. *Ray J. Spies photo, Chicago Historical Society; photo No. ICHi–30733*

BLUE STREAK, CEDAR POINT, SANDUSKY, OHIO

Cedar Point's *Blue Streak* is another John Allen classic. Collaborating with PTC's Frank Hoover, Allen created in 1964 a medium-sized out-and-back coaster that had all the traits of a good ride: smoothness, excellent pacing, airtime on low-lying speed bumps and a spirited race back to the station. Though the *Blue Streak* was recently subjected to a thorough modernization (computer control system, new squeeze brakes, and individual ratcheting lap bars), it is still the preferred woodie at Cedar Point for purists. That's a fair indication of the *Blue Streak* ride experience when you consider that Cedar Point offers an amazing 13 roller coasters from which to choose. On an interesting side note, the *Blue Streak's* name was borrowed from a local Sandusky high school sports team. And, of course, the ride is painted entirely blue. *Mike Schafer*

SWAMP FOX, MYRTLE BEACH, SOUTH CAROLINA

Designed by John Allen and built by PTC for Grand Strand Amusement Park in 1966, the *Swamp Fox* stands only 72 feet tall but is loaded with good drops, fast turns, and several healthy doses of airtime. Situated just a few steps from the Atlantic Ocean, the *Swamp Fox* was rebuilt for the 1992 season when its home park became Family Kingdom. For over ten years, the *Fox* was the only operating seaside woodie other than the Coney Island *Cyclone*. Another interesting fact is that one of this ride's trains is the only surviving component from the long lost Lakeside Park (Virginia) *Shooting Star*. Otto P. Dobnick

the confines of concrete canyons and spread out into the suburbs even farther than they had during the 1920s. This second mass exodus had an adverse and drastic effect on the city amusement parks as urban decay set it.

With patronage progressively declining, rides and park grounds suffered. A sense of shabbiness and perceived danger crept in like a thief in the night and stole the joy and laughter out of what were once safe, happy havens of recreation. The loyal customers who remained feared troublemakers who seemed intent on taking over and mindlessly destroying these once proud places. Parks that had somehow managed to pull through the Great Depression and the two slow decades that followed now found themselves targets of destruction. Some park owners, suffering along

with their vendors from repeated looting and vandalism, saw no recourse other than to get out while they could and closed their parks. Nonetheless, a surprising number of new roller coasters opened in the 1960s. Taking their cue from the success of emerging theme parks, a number of traditional parks changed their operating format, cleaned up their image, or at least added new rides, knowing that a makeover and new attractions drew new crowds. In 1956, Riverview had unveiled plans for a remake for its plain-Jane Miller & Baker *Blue Streak* coaster; those plans became reality in 1960 when the *Fireball* debuted. Also in 1960, the *Skyliner* opened at Roseland Park in Upstate New York's Finger Lakes region. The year 1964 brought new wooden coasters to both Ohio's Cedar Point (the *Blue Streak*) and Denver's Elitch Gardens (*Mister*

Twister). In 1965 Riverview opened a brand-new PTC/John Allen coaster known as the *Jetstream*. In 1967 Lake Winnepesaukah near Chattanooga, Tennessee, yet another John Allen coaster opened, the *Cannon Ball*.

One of the better years for coasterdom during the 1960s was 1968, with four notable coasters rising. At West Mifflin, Pennsylvania, near Pittsburgh, famous Kennywood Park unveiled the incomparable *Thunderbolt*, an in-house designed ride (sidebar). Also in 1968, Seabreeze Park near Rochester, New York, opened an unusual coaster of in-house design called the *Bobsleds*. This ride was, in a sense, ahead of its time, for it featured tubular steel track—at the time possibly the only tubular steel-track coaster in the U.S. outside of Disneyland. Seabreeze's 32-foot-high ride utilized traditional wood structurework and single-car trains not unlike those of *Wild Mouse* rides so popular in the 1950s, and to this day it remains a wonderfully distinctive ride at Seabreeze, a gem of a little traditional park. Also in 1968, Bell's Amusement Park in Tulsa, Oklahoma, opened an out-and-back wood coaster that was pure John Allen. Despite a court order that closes the ride at 9 P.M., *Zingo* has pleased

riders ever since. The ride has an unusual twist that Allen incorporated in some of his other coasters: the longest drop *not* being the first. *Zingo* stands a modest 72 feet high, but its third drop is a breathtaking 86 feet. Like Riverview Park's *Fireball* of yore, the drop dives into an underground tunnel. The fourth 1968 coaster went up at Fairyland Park near Kansas City, Missouri. The creation of veteran designer Aurel Vaszin and NAD, the *Wildcat* had a short life span at this location, closing in 1977. Amazingly, the ride sat dormant for nearly 15 years before being moved, redesigned, and reopened at Frontier City, Oklahoma.

Alas, many of the older parks had been built on what was now deemed prime real estate for something other than an amusement park. Developers wasted little time in buying out weary park owners, and one by one places like Cleveland's Euclid Beach, Chicago's Riverview, St. Louis' Forest Park Highlands, Louisville's Fontaine Ferry Park, and countless others all closed within a few years of each other. The reasons for this decline may have varied from region to region, but the result was the same for so very many amusement parks.

continued on page 107

THE ULTIMATE PRE-RENAISSANCE COASTER PARK

Chicago's famous Riverview Park was a coasterholic's paradise, featuring dozens of different coasters during its 63-year (1904–1967) history, and with as many as 11 coasters operating at a single time. This eastward aerial view shows the park during the 1950s. The thoroughfare at the top of the photo is north-south Western Avenue and at far right is Belmont; the North Branch of the Chicago River is at the bottom. Starting at top of the photo and to the right of the tickets, Riverview's six wood coasters are described, clockwise:

Blue Streak: Of the two lift hills visible at the top center of the photo, the left belongs to this John Miller coaster formerly known as the *Sky Rocket* and rebuilt as the *Fireball* in 1960.

Flash: Near the park's main entrance on Western Avenue is another Miller-inspired ride, the *Flash*. Originally it was the *Pippin*, then the *Silver Streak* (inspired by the new streamlined passenger train, the *Zephyr*, of 1934), then *Silver Flash* after World War II.

Greyhound: This gentle ride, whose south end butted against Belmont Avenue, was razed in 1964 to make way for the John Allen *Jetstream*, which would incorporate some components of the *Greyhound*.

Bobs: The king of Riverview coasters faced the Chicago River. Most of its twisted trackage is visible in this view. A huge racing coaster used to stand immediately east of the *Bobs*.

Flying Turns: Dwarfed by the *Bobs*, the *Flying Turns*—known as the *Kiddie Bobs* when first installed—is immediately to the left of the *Bobs*.

Comet: Tucked in the far northwest corner of the park is yet another Miller ride, originally known as the *Big Dipper* and then the *Zephyr*.

Not shown: *Wild Mouse*, located in the heavily wooded section near the park's center. *Chicago Historical Society, photo No. ICHi-30734; tickets, Mike Schafer collection*

continued from page 103

In the case of Riverview Park—the ultimate coaster park of the pre-coaster renaissance era—the 1967 season concluded with new verbiage on the billboard facing Western Avenue: "Fun for All Ages in 1968; Opens Friday, May 10, 1968." Alas, on October 3, 1967—and under circumstances some insist were prompted by Chicago politics—the park was sold for $6.5 million. The rides were auctioned off in December 1967 and those not purchased by other concerns were leveled. In at least one instance, wreckers used a *Bobs* coaster car as a wrecking ball to demolish the world-famous ride. Of the park's six wood coasters, only the new *Jetstream*—including its colorful, lighted sign—was sold, to Sherwood Park in Rockford, Illinois. Insurance concerns prevented the ride from being rebuilt there, and Sherwood sold the *Jetstream* trains. They wound up at Paramount's Carowinds in Charlotte, North Carolina, where they were used for several years on the *Thunder Road* racing coaster.

Once a park's land was sold, the wrecking crews arrived and unceremoniously leveled some of the most beautiful amusement places—as well as their often innovative wood coasters—that had ever been built. Many of these graceful examples of early twentieth century parks were replaced with faceless high rises (Palisades Park and Euclid Beach), soulless strip malls (Riverview Park), and other commercial developments. Even most of the amusement zone on New York's hallowed Coney Island was not immune to this wholesale destruction as famed Steeplechase Park closed its doors in the mid-1960s. The travesty that so many parks—lovingly built and maintained for generations—could so quickly and shamelessly be wiped out in the name of progress came to be fully realized only during the park and coaster renaissance that would conclude the twentieth century.

Several gems survived the 1960s, notably Kennywood, Elitch Gardens, Denver's Lakeside Park, Santa Cruz Beach and Boardwalk, Cedar Point, Geauga Lake, Idora Park in Youngstown, Ohio, Pittsburgh's famed West View Park, and Pontchartrain Beach in New Orleans, although the last three would succumb during the new roller coaster era that was about to be unleashed at, of all places, a new theme park.

CONEY ISLAND, CINCINNATI

The *Shooting Star* was the undisputed king of all Coney Island coasters. Designed by Herbert Schmeck and built by PTC in 1937, the *Shooting Star* is arguably one of the best out-and-back rides ever built. Schmeck took the existing station and a few other components of the previous resident, PTC's *Clipper*, and fashioned a true legend that became known as the *Shooting Star*. With extra-thick track layering, a steep first drop and downright amazing airtime on several of the lower hills, the *Star* earned the reputation as one of the finest wooden coasters around. But it was perhaps its finale—a wicked hidden plunge into an under-banked tunnel spiral—that helped earn the ride accolades from enthusiasts and the public alike. When it was announced that Coney Island was closing in 1971, and that the *Shooting Star* would *not* be relocated to the new Kings Island theme park, coaster fans lost a true friend. Though Paramount's Canada's Wonderland near Toronto, Ontario, is home to a 1981-built woodie very loosely based on the old Coney ride, it's hardly compares to the original. It is quite surprising that no park owner has taken the initiative and rebuilt this proven classic design true to Schmeck's specifications. If that were to happen, such a park would automatically acquire an instant legend. *David P. Oroszi*

The Coaster Renaissance

5

Steel Coasters Blossom; Wood Coasters Rebound

THE *RACER* AND THE *VORTEX*

Through the coiling loops of the thoroughly modern *Vortex* stands the classic lines of Paramount's Kings Island's *Racer*. Opened in 1972, John Allen's twin-track beauty became the ride that heralded the roller coaster's second golden age. With 3,415 feet of track per side, the 88-foot tall *Racer* offers riders a satisfying collection of low-profile speed hills resulting in plenty of airtime. During the early 1980s, Kings Island started a trend by turning the trains on one of the *Racer*'s track backward. *Otto P. Dobnick*

So very many wonderful old amusement parks and their respective collections of vintage wooden roller coasters were lost during that long, unstable period between the Depression and the end of 1960s. But in 1972, there was an abrupt, almost miraculous reversal in this seemingly indiscriminate wave of devastation. That year symbolized the American roller coaster's true emergence into the second golden age. The catalyst of this historically important event was the well publicized debut of an exciting wooden coaster near Cincinnati, Ohio, called the Racer.

THE COASTER THAT (RE)STARTED IT ALL

Generally regarded as the ride that sparked the roller coaster renaissance, Kings Island's *Racer* opened to rave reviews in 1972 and reaffirmed the importance of roller coasters to amusement parks. The *Racer* was Kings Island's first coaster. Since then, new coasters have blossomed at the southwestern Ohio park, including the renowned *Beast*. As of the new turn of the century, Kings Island boasted no fewer than eight coasters, yet the *Racer* remains a park favorite. *Main photo, Mike Schafer; sign inset, David P. Oroszi*

Designed by John Allen of the Philadelphia Toboggan Company for Kings Island, a brand new theme park north of Cincinnati, this sparkling double-tracked thriller garnered a phenomenal degree of notoriety. The *Racer*'s premier was, without question, a pivotal moment in the history of the roller coaster. The ride's visibility and immediate acceptance gave the amusement industry a much needed shot in the arm. Furthermore, the *Racer* was a sensational ride experience. It seemed as if the media and the public at large simultaneously rediscovered the joy and incomparable excitement that only a well-designed wooden coaster could deliver.

Kings Island opened the year after Cincinnati's renowned Coney Island on the banks of the Ohio River was shuttered at the end of the 1971 season. As one might expect, there was a great deal of sentiment attached to Coney Island. Like other regional parks, the grand old place had been an integral part of area life for generations. But the Ohio river's perennial flooding was costly, and Coney itself had been through one too many disasters. The park's owners were aware that with growing crowds, more land was needed for expansion and the old apple orchard adjacent to the unpredictable river was no longer a practical option. Kings Island was the compromise.

Like other theme parks gaining popularity around the nation, Kings Island could never truly replace the traditional charm and spirit the predecessor it replaced. But at least in this case, Old Coney would not die in vain. Developers wisely devoted an entire section of the new park to pay homage to Coney Island. They moved many of Coney's "iron rides"— *Tilt-A-Whirls*, *Scramblers*, Ferris wheels, and the like—to Kings Island and placed them before the true star of the new park—the *Racer*.

Following Kings Island's lead, a slew of new themers followed suit by incorporating sensational new wooden roller coasters into their ride arsenals. PTC's John Allen and his associates churned out an impressive number of contemporary rides for this new crop of eager customers. Six Flags Over Georgia got the picturesque *Great American Scream Machine* (1973) while *Racer*-inspired cousins were installed at Kings Dominion (*Rebel Yell*, 1975) and Carowinds

(*Thunder Road*, 1976). Six Flags Over Mid-America became home home to Allen's final coaster in 1976, the *Screamin' Eagle*. Wooden coasters began their comeback on the West Coast when Magic Mountain debuted International Amusement Device's final coaster—the twin-tracked *Colossus*—in 1978.

Business was booming, and these new theme parks built successively larger and more impressive wooden coasters. At the same time, those traditional parks which had somehow managed to survive were benefiting enormously from this renewed interest in outdoor entertainment. Amusement parks were once again fashionable, and those smaller venues which had fastidiously maintained their classic wooden coasters knew they had a unique and marketable product of which the new theme parks simply could not boast: nostalgia.

Smithsonian-Endorsed Coasters

Taking particular note of the rekindled interest in roller coasters once again sweeping across North America was industry historian and author Dr. Robert Cartmell. Then an assistant professor in art and printmaking at the State University of New York at Albany, Cartmell penned a New York *Times* article in 1974 entitled "The Quest for the Ultimate Roller Coaster." This now-legendary morsel of literature focused on the importance and impact of the roller coaster in American history. It gave a teasing peek at the amusement industry's colorful legacy and made note of the immeasurable loss suffered when some of the greatest wooden roller coasters ever built were demolished during the four decades following the Great Depression. This article also listed the names and locations of several notable classic coasters still in operation along with Cartmell's

Smithsonian Institution
TOP TEN COASTERS
1 THUNDERBOLT, KENNYWOOD, PITTSBURGH
2 MISTER TWISTER, ELITCH'S, DENVER
3 CYCLONE, CONEY ISLAND, NEW YORK
4 GREAT AMERICAN SCREAM MACHINE, SIX FLAGS, ATLANTA
5 RACER (LA MONTANA RUSA) CHAPULTEPEC PARK, MEXICO CITY
6 GIANT COASTER, PARAGON PARK BOSTON
7 COMET, CRYSTAL BEACH, ONTARIO, CANADA
8 REBEL YELL, KINGS DOMINION, ASHLAND, VA.
9 GIANT DIPPER, SEASIDE SANTA CRUZ CALIF.
10 COASTER, DORNEY PARK, ALLENTOWN, PA.

THE SMITHSONIAN'S TOP TEN

This sign placed at the entranceway to Kennywood Park's *Thunderbolt* presented the top ten coaster list of the esteemed Smithsonian Institution at the dawn of the 1980s. *Mike Schafer*

own personal "Top Ten" compilation of what he considered the best rides out there.

That single dissertation ignited a virtual firestorm of
interest. Frenzied correspondence from coaster fans
around the world commenced. In Cartmell's own
book published in 1987, *The Incredible Scream
Machine—A History of the Roller Coaster*, he men-
tions being overwhelmed by more than 8,000 writers
who contacted him expressing their emphatic interest
and love of these wonderful rides. Nearly each letter
carried the same message: Cartmell's influential article
had made them aware that there were thousands of
other people out there who shared a passion for this
marvelous machine called the roller coaster.

Perhaps inspired by this extraordinary response to
the public's admission of roller coaster enthusiasm,
the Smithsonian Institution, in conjunction with Cartmell, sponsored and launched a traveling exhibition in

1976 dubbed "Coast-To-Coast Coasters." This display contained 265 photos of vintage and contemporary coasters along with descriptive text focusing on
the ride's evolution. For several years, this popular
production toured 75 U.S. cities, drawing from the
closet hundreds of individuals who shared a common
love and devotion to roller coasters. The exhibit also
educated and made the American public aware of the
important role the roller coaster has played in our
recreational history. Newspapers across the country
picked up on the unusual subject, and suddenly roller
coasters were thrust further into the public limelight.

Mine Trains to Loopers: the Steel Coaster Evolution

Based on the ultra-successful technology devised
for Disneyland's *Matterhorn Bobsleds* in 1959, Arrow
Development refined and improved the concept and

THE *SHOOTING STAR*, SALEM, VIRGINIA

This view from the top of the first drop of the *Shooting Star* at Lakeside Park near Roanoke, Virginia, shows the typical out-and-back format of a classic renaissance-era John Allen coaster. As was often the case with these early renaissance rides, the coaster formed a spectacular backdrop to the rest of the park and an enticing invitation for excitement. Unfortunately, since this 1985 photo was recorded, Lakeside Park has been closed and the *Shooting Star* dismantled. *Otto P. Dobnick*

COLOSSUS

A mountain of lumber, *Colossus* could be considered the first "mega coaster," but it was also the last coaster built by International Amusement Devices, the successor to venerable manufacturer National Amusement Device, Inc. *Colossus* opened at Magic Mountain outside Los Angeles in 1978, and its sheer size made it popular fodder for the news media—not to mention the perfect prop for the Chevy Chase farce, *National Lampoon's Vacation*. The publicity was not all good: An accident closed the ride briefly for modifications which resulted in the ride's taming. *Otto P. Dobnick.*

opened the next generation tubular-steel track roller coaster at Six Flags Over Texas in 1966. Called the *Runaway Mine Train*, this was the first coaster in which renowned designer Ron Toomer was involved. After successfully working out a number of technical bugs, Toomer and his associates at Arrow unleashed the *Mine Train* prototype to rave reviews.

The ride featured a more complex version of the tubular steel rail/polyurethane wheel setup, but in many ways mimicked the action of wooden roller coasters. The *Runaway Mine Train* had three lift hills and several multiple-car trains. Six Flags over Texas was another full-fledged theme park that had recently opened, and it needed a high-capacity ride able to handle the crowds that were growing larger

with each season. The *Runaway Mine Train* filled that need.

Passengers boarded ore-car-themed trains and embarked on a tight and twisted track layout comprised of banked curves, surprise drops, and quick directional changes. The ride's finale consisted of the train climbing the third lift, passing through a distracting saloon replica and suddenly plunging down into a dark curving tunnel. This rollicking ending whisked giddy riders beneath a man made lagoon before gliding smoothly up into the station house.

As hoped, the general public embraced the exciting new experience and Six Flags, along with a number of other growing theme park's around the country, inundated Arrow with requests for their very own Mine Trains. Arrow stepped up to the challenge and delivered the product. The *Matterhorn Bobsleds* and most of the early mine-train-type coasters are still in operation today.

Following Arrow's trailblazing lead in steel coaster technology, ride manufacturers around the world began developing their own versions of the tubular steel track roller coaster. From the Asia to Europe (especially Germany and Switzerland), an amazing assortment of companies entered into the lucrative steel coaster market. Many of those foreign rides made their way to North America, continuously challenging U.S. designers to evolve and improve their product.

While Germany's Anton Schwarzkopf developed his *Wild Cat* and *Jet Star* compact steel coasters, firms like Italy's Pinfari introduced their incredibly popular *Galaxy*. Examples of all these early steel roller coasters can still be found in operation at permanent parks and traveling shows the world over.

MINE-TRAIN COASTERS

Shown in 1980, the *Runaway Mine Train* opened at Six Flags Great Adventure, Jackson, New Jersey, in 1974. The hills are gentle and the swoops are smooth, thereby providing a ride that the whole family can enjoy. The new "mine-train" coasters of the late 1960s and early 1970s were, in fact, simply a new breed of the scenic railways that had delighted millions during the early years of the twentieth century. *Mike Schafer*

GALAXY STEEL COASTER

Overshadowed by its newer wooden cousin, the twin-track *Rebel Yell*, in this 1984 photo, a Pinfari-produced *Galaxy* basks in the Virginia sun for its last season at Kings Dominion. These all-metal rides utilized steel girder rails, two-car trains, and a helix-dominated track layout. Technically a portable ride, *Galaxy* coasters can be found around the world and are popular at major state fairs, although several U.S. parks have them as permanent installations. *Otto P. Dobnick*

Upside-Down Coastering

It had been nearly a century since roller coaster designers had attempted to send courageous riders through an upside-down element. The primitive and short-lived looping coaster experiments at parks in North America and Europe around the beginning of the twentieth century were doomed for lack of any safety devices as well as loop configurations that were uncomfortable to riders. Low passenger capacity was the final straw for those early inverters.

But in the mid 1970s, the amusement industry approached the looping coaster concept armed with advanced mathematics and a determination to give the thrillseeking public something new and unusual. In a relatively short period of time, steel coaster manufacturers had gained invaluable knowledge and experience with tubular steel rails and various nylon/polyurethane wheeled trains. Their work on rides like the *Runaway Mine Train* (Arrow Development), *Wild Cats*, and *Jet Stars* (Anton Schwarzkopf), among others, was about to pay off in a big, big way.

With this new technology, coasters were able to go faster, have steeper drops, and feature curves banked at nearly 90 degrees. These modern industry pioneers knew that with powerful computers and the superior steel-bending techniques available to them, the sky was quite literally the limit as to what they could do increase the thrill factor. The next logical step was sending riders upside down.

Contemporary engineers had closely researched the early looping rides, recognized their flaws, and devised their own new and improved versions which actually worked. Arrow had been working on the loop concept for several years, but instead of starting out with a vertical loop, engineers instead devised a barrel-roll maneuver and called the resulting ride the *Corkscrew*. This sensational coaster opened to great fanfare at California's Knott's Berry Farm in 1975. It was an instant success.

The first successful vertical looping coaster was built at California's Magic Mountain in 1976. Through a collaboration between Germany's Anton Schwarzkopf's company and Intamin AG of Switzerland, this wondrous new marvel was also an immediate hit. Aptly dubbed the *Revolution*, this polished

THE *CORKSCREW*, KNOTT'S BERRY FARM

Tubular steel-track coasters allowed for acrobatics that previously had been thought to be impossible. Arrow Development's prototype *Corkscrew* was the ride from which numerous duplicates were created for parks all over North America. Most of those rides built in the mid-1970s are still in operation in one location or another. The Knott's *Corkscrew* was dismantled and moved to Silverwood Theme Park, Athol, Idaho, where it today is entertaining a new generation of thrillseekers. *Otto P. Dobnick*

Shuttle Loopers

The term "shuttle loop" refers to a type of steel roller coaster featuring a single train that is propelled through a series of inversions both backward and forward over the same stretch of track.

The first shuttle loop was developed by Intamin AG and Anton Schwarzkopf for Kings Dominion (Virginia) in 1977. Called the *King Kobra*, this innovative ride's 28-passenger train was dramatically launched along a flat plane into a 90-foot vertical loop and then up a 138-foot tall ramp that ended abruptly in mid-air. Once the train lost momentum (before the end of track), it fell 13 stories backward and flew back through the loop. After ripping past the station and up a smaller reversing ramp, riders returned to the loading platform. Total ride time was less than a minute but deliciously intense.

This coaster's propulsion system was relatively simple: a 40-ton weight attached to a system of cables and pulleys was released down a hollow tube (which also served as the support structure for the taller ramp section). A dolly mechanism connected to the cable made contact with the train and effectively pushed it along the launch corridor as the weight dropped. Later versions of this shuttle loop utilized a more efficient flywheel/cable/clutch unit to the blast the train from the station. Both devices produce the exhilarating sensation a fighter pilot feels when his jet rockets off an aircraft carrier at sea.

During the same period, Arrow Development came up with its own variation of the shuttle loop. Instead of vertical reverse points, riders hike five stories to a lofty loading platform. Once seated in the train, they are propelled out of the station via a cable system. An abrupt drop leads into a vertical loop and a rapid ascent to a dead-end horizontal stretch of track (identical to the station area on the opposite end of the narrow ride.). After a brief pause, the train is launched backward through the course to the starting point.

In 1984, Dutch ride-builder Vekoma devised a triple looping shuttle called the *Boomerang*. On this ride, the train is hoisted backward out of the station up a steep 125-foot hill via a cable lift system. After the cars are released, they plow through the station, into a double looping boomerang element, a vertical loop, and up a steep reverse ramp positioned against the first tower. A chain drive briskly pulls the train to its highest point

MONTEZUMA'S REVENGE SHUTTLE LOOP

Riders on the *Montezuma's Revenge* shuttle loop at Knott's Berry Farm are catapulted through a vertical loop and up toward the end of track. *Terry Lind*

before releasing it through the course in reverse. (Vekoma recently introduced this same device with inverted, feet-dangling trains. It was affectionately dubbed *Invertigo*.)

The most outrageous shuttle around is the hyper-intense *Weiner Looping* that Schwarzkopf built for the Prater (Vienna, Austria) in 1982. This wonderfully terrifying contraption uses a friction tire-drive system for propulsion. With the elevated station located in the center of the compact layout, the train is drawn backward out of the station to the top of the first 13-story tower. When the drive reverses direction, it shoots riders through the station, around a severely banked turn, and through a vertical loop encircling the loading platform. A reversing tower launches victims screaming through the whole thing again—backward.

Chapter 6 provides additional coverage of "New Age" shuttles, but in the mean time, examples of all the above-mentioned thrillers are still in operation and just waiting for a new generation of daredevils.

MULTI-INVERSION COASTER

The *Viper* at Six Flags Magic Mountain in Valencia, California illustrates the classic multi-inversion steel coaster of the 1980s. Following a twisting drop off the lift hill, trains enter a lofty vertical loop followed by a sweeping curve that leads to two consecutive vertical loops. Beyond, trains enter a complex element (to the left of the main part of the coaster) known as a "boomerang." The ride concludes with a traditional double barrel roll (corkscrew). *Terry Lind*

thriller was a long, graceful ride and an amazing engineering accomplishment. Schwarzkopf's approach differed considerably in its wheel assembly, track, and vehicle design, but the coaster achieved the same goal: it sent riders head over heels. The *Revolution* even "starred" in Universal's *Rollercoaster* in 1977. The film gave the entire world a glimpse of the latest word in amusement ride technology.

Park owners were ecstatic as these phenomenal new machines drew crowds in record numbers. The introduction of the looping coasters ignited a virtual arms race of steel roller coaster building that continues

to this day. Over the next several years, steel roller coasters began to get taller, faster, and more extravagant. Arrow, Intamin/Schwarzkopf, and a handful of other international and domestic manufacturers came up with various incarnations of steel coasters incorporating the loop/corkscrew configuration.

Arrow and Intamin went head to head by each offering their own versions of the unique "shuttle Loop" coaster (sidebar). Though they differed in their execution, both versions featured trains that were catapulted forward through a single vertical loop and up an incline—then backward through the loop.

In addition to steel coasters growing exponentially in height and length, the number of inversions began to increase, and designers were continuously pressured to come up with new ways to turn riders upside down. Fierce-sounding maneuvers like "sidewinders," "boomerangs," "cutbacks," and other

THE *SHOCK WAVE*, TEXAS STYLE

Among the early renaissance contestants for intense steel coasters was the Schwarzkopf-designed *Shock Wave* at Six Flags Over Texas between Dallas and Fort Worth. Opened in 1978 along with a sister ride, the *Mind Bender*, at Six Flags Over Georgia, this 116-foot-high ride, shown in July 1982, features a set of double vertical loops so intense that many riders often experience a momentary blackout while the trains fly through the double inversion. There are also moments of negative Gs—something unusual for a steelie. *Mike Schafer*

FLASHBACK—THE "HAIRPIN DROP" COASTER

As the 1980s unfolded, coaster manufacturers went into high gear with new ideas of how to twist tubular-steel track. Although it never quite caught on, one interesting experiment to come from Intamin AG was a semi-portable coaster that featured 180-degree hairpin drops at each end of the ride, plus an upward 540-degree corkscrew. The ride opened first at Six Flags Great America near Chicago in 1985 where it was known as *Z-Force*. Once its "shelf life" had expired there, it was moved to Six Flags Over Georgia in 1988, and finally to Six Flags Magic Mountain in California where it was renamed *Flashback*. Though the inversions are intense, the ride suffers a mite from slow pacing between the radical elements. Though Intamin still offers the ride for sale, this is the only version ever manufactured. *Six Flags*

The Organized Coaster Fan

Several roller coaster fan clubs have sprung up during the great coaster renaissance that was sparked by the opening of the *Racer* at Kings Island in 1972. First, best known, and biggest is the American Coaster Enthusiasts, founded in 1978. ACE has evolved into the world's largest club of roller coaster enthusiasts. With 6,000-plus members representing 49 states, Washington, D.C., and 12 countries, this eclectic group's prime directive is to foster and promote the conservation, appreciation, knowledge, and enjoyment of wooden and steel roller coasters.

The group's origins can be traced back to 1977, when three young men participated in a roller coaster marathon organized as a publicity stunt to promote the motion picture *Rollercoaster*. During and after that event, which took place on the *Rebel Yell* at Kings Dominion in Virginia, the threesome tossed around the idea of forming a club of roller coaster buffs.

To accomplish the task, they collected from other coaster fans and amusement parks the names and addresses of individuals who were enamored by roller coasters. Over the ensuing winter, this resourceful trio sent out blind invitations to the enthusiasts on their list and announced a gathering to be held at Busch Gardens in Williamsburg, Virginia, in June 1978. That park just happened to be opening the world's biggest looping roller coaster at the same time.

The rapid response to their simple query was overwhelming, to say the least. There were far more people out there with an intense love of these marvelous thrill rides than anyone had ever imagined. That now-legendary gathering became known as Coaster Con 1, and it brought together an incredibly enthusiastic, diverse group of people (including this book's author) of all ages from all over North America.

The cement that binds together the American Coaster Enthusiasts (ACE) is the club's quarterly color magazine, *Roller Coaster!*, and its bimonthly *Ace News* newsletter.

That first convention, where ACE was officially organized, gave the approximately 50 attendees the chance to share individual coaster experiences, display photo and postcard collections, and even view film and video of grand old amusement parks and lost coasters that were no longer in operation. It was an incredible time of learning, fellowship, and, of course, coaster riding.

Busch Gardens allowed the group to visit the park when it was closed to the public and enjoy ACE's very first "ERT" (exclusive ride time) aboard the incredible *Loch Ness Monster*, the record-breaking looper that remains today one of the most popular steel coasters around.

Every year since then, ACE's membership has grown, and it has become a respected authority on the subject of roller coasters. Because of the group's combined research efforts, a more complete picture of the amusement industry's colorful history has been documented and assembled. There are still plenty of coaster mysteries and legends out there, so the research is ongoing.

ACE has also been instrumental in rallying support for and bringing attention to certain classic wooden coasters in danger of being destroyed. In some instances, such as the those involving the *Giant Dipper* at San Diego's Belmont Park and Lakemont Park's *Leap the Dips* in Altoona, Pennsylvania, ACE was a critical component of the rescue and restoration process.

In essence, ACE is a fan club for roller coaster lovers, but besides the benefits to which the yearly membership fee entitles them (informative and educational publications, numerous organized events at parks with ERT aboard their coasters, and a host of other perks), the club gives people who share a common interest the chance to celebrate together that great American thrill device known as the roller coaster.

Website: www.ACEonline.org

Bisly's Spiral Airship, Long Beach, Cal.
The only one in the world.

Suspendeds and Stand Ups and More Shuttles, Oh My!

The dawn of the 1980s found steel-coaster designers virtually repeating history. Like their counterparts back in the Roaring Twenties, these engineering renegades were eager to push the envelope beyond the norm, constantly challenging the unforgiving laws of gravity by devising innovative ways to scare the heck out of park guests. And just as their own ancestors were prone to do, modern park guests would climb aboard just about anything their local fun spot could build. Fear and the illusion of danger have always been powerful intoxicants.

But by this point, no matter how it was packaged, the mere aspect of simply traveling upside down was no longer a novelty. Just as their grandparents or

stomach-churning elements comprised these seemingly otherworldly machines, and eventually any ride designer worth his or her illustrious name was incorporating as many of these elements as could be reasonably be fitted within a single ride. As expected, the fearless public remained true to its nature; people clamored for a chance to experience the latest and greatest, always asking for more.

EARLY SUSPENDED COASTER

As this early twentieth century postcard suggests, the idea of a suspended coaster is hardly new. The *Spiral Airship* at Long Beach, California, featured individual cars that were hoisted to the top of the lift hill and then released into a spiral section of track in which they "circled" in for a landing. Then, as now, the fact that suspended coasters mimic certain flight patterns was not lost upon designers. *George Siessel*

THE *BAT*, KINGS ISLAND

Despite the ride depicted above at Long Beach, Kings Island claimed its *Bat* to be the first suspended coaster in the world—and at the time of its 1982 unveiling, it likely was the *only* suspended coaster in the world. Those fortunate enough to have experienced this cleverly themed but short-lived ride insist the *Bat* was one of the best steel coasters ever. Note the extreme swing of the cars in relation to the overhead track. Struts—visible flanking the main suspension arms on which the cars are attached—were necessary to dampen the snap of those arms as trains flung around curves. Alas, teething problems too numerous to address in a retrofit resulted in the *Bat* being dismantled. *Kings Island*

BIG BAD WOLF SUSPENDED COASTER

Once the bugs had been eliminated from the intricacies of suspended-coaster technology, successful rides sprang up. One of the earliest and most successful is the *Big Bad Wolf* at Busch Gardens Williamsburg in Williamsburg, Virginia. *Big Bad Wolf* trains hurtle through woods and a village that has been "abandoned" on account of a terrorizing beast. In one of the most frightening ride finales ever devised, trains suddenly plunge toward a river at warp speed, flinging passengers outward as they hurtle around the bend just above the water's surface. *Otto P. Dobnick*

parents had grown tired of the simple *Scenic Railways* and side-friction coasters, late twentieth century patrons quickly tired of the loopers and demanded something new, something different. Urged by park owners eager to please paying customers, designers scrambled for new coaster concepts. Arrow was once again at the forefront when it introduced the first successful suspended coaster in 1982 at Kings Island.

Called the *Bat*, this fascinating prototype featured seven-car trains hanging from an overhead track. Trains of basically free-swinging four-passenger vehicles gave riders a real and sometimes frightening sample of a bat's erratic flight pattern. Though this amazing new coaster was indeed thrilling, it was also plagued with mechanical problems. Downtime was

frequent as Arrow engineers tried to fine tune their new baby in the field.

As is the case with many prototypes, unforeseen complications arose. The unpredictable nature of the cars' swinging action added unusual dynamics to the typical roller coaster equation. The *Bat* operated sporadically for two years before being dismantled in favor of a more reliable multi-looping coaster system (Arrow's six-inversion *Vortex,* built on the site of the *Bat* and utilizing the old *Bat* station; the *Vortex* remains a staple of Kings Island's coaster fleet).

Arrow, however, had learned plenty from the *Bat*. By solving a number of technical problems that involved track banking and the degree of vehicle swing that could be tolerated, Arrow developed a

COASTER FEVER
Model Coasters

JOHN A. HUNT, COASTER MODELER

New Yorker John Hunt has been building coaster models for decades. Here at an American Coaster Enthusiast's convention, John displays his miniature works of art.

As with any other hobby, roller coaster enthusiasm is celebrated in many forms. Some folks capture these complex machines on film or video, some draw or paint their favorite subject, while others are content to simply ride. And some build models of them.

For New York's John A. Hunt, the meticulous process is more pleasurable than challenging—John has been building coaster models since childhood. Growing up in Boston, John developed a strong affinity for amusement parks and his favorite attraction, the roller coaster. His father frequently took young John to Revere Beach—in its heyday, Boston's answer to New York's Coney Island. It was once home to several legendary roller coasters, including the Fred Church–designed *Cyclone*. It was then that John Hunt began a lifelong love affair with roller coasters.

Though too young to ride that *Cyclone* before it and all the Revere amusements closed forever, he did experience each and every coaster he could during subsequent family outings to other New England parks. On these trips he closely examined the coasters' structure and equipment to find out just what made them tick. His determined interest in these mechanical wonders motivated him to create miniature versions of the rides.

His early endeavors, he admits, were a bit crude. Fashioned of cardboard, paper, and glue, they were just the beginning. Over the years, John nurtured and honed his craft, and as he grew older, he discovered other roller coasters across the country. An episode of a popular children's TV program featuring the venerable Coney Island *Cyclone* mesmerized him and really set his model building into motion. He has since constructed many copies of the Coney Island *Cyclone*—for himself, for friends, and for customers. He has recreated such legendary classics as the *Cyclone Racer*, the Lincoln Park *Comet*, Revere Beach's *Cyclone*

and *Lightning*, and the Crystal Beach *Cyclone*. He has also built models of currently operating coasters like the *Phoenix*, *Texas Giant*, *Riverside Cyclone*, and *Roar*.

John's portfolio of coaster models may be viewed on his website at: www.rollercoastermodels.com. A section even depicts the entire construction process.

As a member of the American Coaster Enthusiasts, John has been able to ride more than 300 coasters throughout North America. During his travels, his inspiration and devotion to model building grew stronger while his proficiency improved dramatically. He has built dozens of roller coaster models and even has several on permanent display at museums and amusement parks: *Flyer Comet* (Whalom Park Historical Museum, Lunenburg, Massachusetts); *Sky Princess* (Dutch Wonderland, Lancaster, Pennsylvania); and *Leap The Dips* (Lakemont Park Historical Museum, Altoona, Pennsylvania).

second-generation suspended coaster, and it worked like a charm.

Two examples of the improved version opened in 1984: The *Big Bad Wolf* at Busch Gardens in Williamsburg, Virginia, and *XLR8* (say it fast) at AstroWorld in Houston, Texas. These two attractions clearly illustrated the reliability of Arrow's improved suspended-coaster technology, and they, as well as several others which followed, are scattered around the world and still in operation today.

The year 1984 also saw the introduction of Vekoma's *Boomerang* coaster. This triple-looping shuttle loop (six inversions if you count the fact that riders experience the same layout in reverse) became one of history's most widely produced off-the-shelf steel roller coasters.

That same year, the pioneering Kings Island opened North America's first "stand-up coaster," the *King Kobra*. A product of Japanese manufacturer Togo, the ride featured a relatively simple layout with the added punch of a vertical loop. Intamin later introduced their own version of a stand-up coaster at

Magic Mountain. The ride was actually designed by Swiss ride-builder Giavinola and called the *Shockwave*. This layout was longer and a bit more convoluted and featured a single vertical loop. Perhaps what made the *Shockwave* especially unique was the masterful engineering involved in the design. Besides the ride's precise attention to detail in its fabrication, the trains featured an unusual four-across seating (standing, actually) configuration. Things were once more beginning to get very interesting.

Also in 1984 Intamin unveiled a re-creation of the

Flying Turns, a trackless toboggan ride invented by Canadian Norman Bartlett in the 1920s (chapter 2). Instead of employing the original ride's trough construction of pliable cypress wood, the new coaster's channel was fashioned of steel. Riders were seated in large, cumbersome sled-shaped vehicles instead of trains. The ride was a quite a bit tamer than its predecessor, but it still offered guests a decent simulation of summertime bobsledding.

German manufacturer Mack entered the race with its own version of the *Flying Turns* which opened as the *Avalanche* at Kings Dominion. Mack's variation featured multi-car trains traveling in a steel trough and overall more closely resembled the appearance and action of those *Flying Turns* of yore. Several examples of the Intamin and Mack rides are in operation today at parks in the U.S. and abroad, but legendary accounts of the relentless, freewheeling ride qualities of the original rides cause enthusiasts to long for someone to rebuild one of the wooden variety.

In 1988 Arrow Dynamics took the looping coaster to the next level. The firm built the first of three monstrous multi-looping coasters at Six Flags Great America (Gurnee, Illinois, between Chicago and Milwaukee). This ride was the biggest looping coaster to date and offered a mind-numbing seven inversions. Two similar seven-loop versions subsequently opened at Six Flags Great Adventure (1989) at Jackson, New Jersey, and Six Flags Magic Mountain (1990) outside of Los Angeles.

So Who Builds These Things?

New roller coasters have been blossoming all over during the great coaster renaissance that began in 1972, but they just didn't pop out of the ground on their own, of course. Someone had to plant the seeds and then nurture their growth. As was the case during the first golden age of roller coasters, a number of individuals and companies today specialize in the design and construction of coasters.

By the 1970s, notable coaster designers and firms had dwindled to, basically, National Amusement Device and John Allen and his Philadelphia Toboggan Company. But the ensuing boom changed all that, and since 1972 a plethora of designers and manufacturers have entered the marketplace, taking part in the construction of hundreds of new rides—more than we can fully document on the confines of these pages. In some cases these people and companies have also rebuilt old classics of the golden age.

Renaissance Designers and Firms: Wood-Track Coasters

John Allen

John Allen is reverently referred to as the direct link between the first golden age of roller coasters and the current boom ignited by his own *Racer* in 1972. Allen's esteemed career in the amusement industry began during the Great Depression. Working as a troubleshooter for PTC, he toiled alongside many active roller coaster artists of that era, absorbing what each of them had to offer and honing his own skills in this highly specialized craft. This was especially true of his association with PTC's master designer Herbert Schmeck. One of Allen's early contributions was his involvement with PTC's 1947 transformation of Harry Traver's notorious Crystal Beach *Cyclone* into the amazing *Comet*. The success of the *Comet* project gave Allen a chance to shine in the eyes of his peers, and in 1954 he became president of PTC.

Over the next quarter century, Allen's signature appeared on approximately 25 roller coaster installations. Just as every designer exhibits his own individual style, Allen's personal technique sang of graceful, non-jarring drops and smooth turns. He tended to shy away from the rough-and-tumble classics PTC and other firms produced in the early years. He was a meticulous engineer who made every effort to provide his clients with a well-built and relatively trouble-free product. Though his discriminating methods were sometimes criticized, he was unfazed. He simply did not like a wild ride.

Allen designed a number of entertaining rides; aside from Kings Island's *Racer*, Allen was the creator of *Mister Twister* (1964 and 1965, Denver, Colorado), the *Swamp Fox* (1966, Myrtle Beach, South Carolina), *Zingo* (1968, Tulsa, Oklahoma), *Rebel Yell* (1975, Richmond, Virginia), the *Great American Scream Machine* (1973, Atlanta, Georgia), and the *Screamin' Eagle* (1976, St. Louis, Missouri) among

others. Truly an instrumental force, he was the man who was almost single handedly responsible for helping to keep the roller coaster alive and well during the industry's darkest years.

John Allen died in 1979, the same year that PTC stopped building roller coasters and concentrated mainly on train construction. He was the last active coaster designer from the early days, and one may be inclined to surmise that this important bridge to the past would spell the end of of his influence. Fortunately, that was not the case. Over the years, he had imparted his esteemed knowledge in coaster design to other enterprising individuals, such as William Cobb.

William H. Cobb

Following the passing of John Allen, the torch was figuratively handed over to Texas-based civil engineer William Cobb. Cobb had been initiated into the amusement industry in 1961 during the opening of Six Flags Over Texas. The soft-spoken Texan became associated with Allen over the years while working as structural engineer on such popular rides as *The Great American Scream Machine* and *Screamin' Eagle*. After Allen's death, Cobb's creative genius seemed to kick into high gear. He went on to create a series of wooden coasters that often contrasted rather dramatically with

continued on page 128

DELMAS SEVIER, FROM MAINTENANCE TO DESIGN

Delmas Sevier, wooden coaster engineer for Six Flags theme parks is shown in 1990 checking the track gauge (distance between rails) on the Curtis Summers-designed *Texas Giant* at Six Flags Over Texas. Keeping proper spacing between a coaster's rails ensures that the train doesn't "hunt" (slam back and forth as it struggles to remain on course). Maintenance crews pay extra attention to track gauging, as this translates into a smoother ride for guests and less wear and tear on the coaster trains and structure. *Gary Slade*

WILLIAM H. COBB

Congenial and mild-mannered, Bill Cobb seemed hardly the type to have produced such wild woodies as his two most notable *Cyclones*, the *Texas Cyclone* at Houston and the Riverside *Cyclone* near Springfield, Massachusetts. Interestingly, account of a heart condition, he was never able to ride some of his creations. *Gary Slade*

125

Coaster Stations

FLYER STATION, HOLYOKE, MASSACHUSETTS

Buck Rogers would feel right at home boarding the *Flyer* at now-defunct Mountain Park near Holyoke, Massachusetts. *Mike Schafer*

BIG COASTER STATION, ARNOLDS PARK, IOWA

Funky is the keyword for the *Big Coaster* station at this park. Not only does the station pass above a pedestrian way, but it does double duty supporting the fun house. *Mike Schafer*

The gateway to a roller coaster ride is its loading station. Like their railway counterparts, these structures can range from the perfunctory to the elaborate, sublime to otherworldly. The station usually sets the tone for the ride experience ahead ... usually.

Pictured at right, the Lakeside *Cyclone*'s station is an Art Deco confection of flowing angles and dreamy indirect lighting. A flight aboard the *Cyclone* itself reflects these attributes perfectly—it is a ride of sweeping drops and graceful turns, incandescent chase lights and pastel hues, all splashed with a sensual 1940s flavor. The *Cyclone*, as well as all of Denver's Lakeside Park, amounts to a little slice of heaven for the artist and thrillseeker in each of us.

On the other hand, many steel coaster stations seem like sentinels to the respective metal gods they serve. Most of these are sleek, streamlined and airy utilitarian buildings designed expressly as no-nonsense portals to futuristic hyper-thrillers. Take the station built for Cedar Point's *Magnum XL200*, for example. This open-air concrete platform topped by a simple roof is minimal at best. Its purpose is simply to provide a shelter for the operators who continually process the three 36-passenger trains. *Magnum* requires no pomp or circumstance in its accouterments.

Then we have that other category: the innocuous coaster station that hides the true nature of the creature you're about to tackle. A good example is the *Outer Limits: Flight of Fear* LIM coasters at Paramount's Kings Island and Kings Dominion. During each ride's indoor Hangar 18 pre-show, guests are drawn into a top secret storyline that commands their attention. The actual coaster structure is kept hidden away in another part of the attraction. Once seated in the coaster train and launched from the space-age platform, passengers are completely unprepared for the tumultuous, multi-looping journey that awaits.

In the same vein, the station for the *Beast* at Paramount's Kings Island is a rustic wooden structure fashioned of huge timbers and sporting a nostalgic nineteenth century mining theme. Again, other than this mysterious coaster's first lift hill, little else of the ride is visible from inside the park. First-time riders departing the *Beast*'s relatively simple station are frequently blown away by the 35-acre thriller deceptively hidden within the park's forested hills and ravine.

So, whether you like your stations decked out like some ornate Victorian railway palace or wrapped up in the cocoon-like calm of deep-space, you're bound to find something out there to suit your particular tastes. Each roller coaster offers something unique in its ride experience, so it's only fitting that the designer should extend that flavor to the attraction's heart—the station.

Besides the examples of roller coaster stations mentioned in this

section, there are few other favorites that tend to rate highly with enthusiasts who take pleasure in the architectural aspects of a roller coaster as well as the adrenaline-pumping physical sensations. In no particular order: the old-fashioned railway theme of the *Lisebergbahn* non-looping steel (Liserberg Park, Gothenberg, Sweden); the over-the-top medieval castle for *Dueling Dragons* inverted coasters (Islands of Adventure, Orlando, Florida); the soft lighting and functional woodwork of the beautiful *Racer* (Kennywood Park, Pittsburgh); the archeological/Egyptian splendor of the inverted *Montu* (Busch Gardens Tampa Bay); and any of the outer space-themed *Space Mountain* steel coasters at the Disney Parks.

CYCLONE STATION, LAKESIDE PARK, DENVER

What is arguably the most classic coaster station ever is this Art Deco masterpiece serving the equally classic *Cyclone* coaster at Denver's Lakeside Park. On this warm summer evening in 1982, the colorful glow and smooth lines of this wonderful structure jettisons park-goers back to the Big Band era. *Mike Schafer*

LE MONSTRE, MONTREAL

Though Bill Cobb designed relatively few coasters, most of those he did are highly regarded. His only racing coaster was truly a monster, and was aptly christened *Le Monstre*. It resides at La Ronde, an amusement park on an island (the site of Expo '67) in the middle of the St. Lawrence River in Montreal, Quebec. *Le Monstre* is an unusual racing coaster in that the two tracks rarely follow the same profile yet the trains somehow manage to end up on the station brakes at approximately the same time. *La Ronde*

continued from page 125

Allen's style of relatively gentle though entertaining designs. In a couple of instances, they were downright wild.

Cobb's most famous work is the *Texas Cyclone* which opened at Houston's AstroWorld in 1976. He was asked to produce a modern version of New York's illustrious Coney Island *Cyclone* after the park's plans to purchase that famous ride fell through. When the *Texas Cyclone* opened, it was hailed by many as the greatest modern wooden coaster on the planet. Though the *Texas Cyclone* turned out just as intended, this over-the-top thriller

was extreme—riding the back seat required seat belts in addition to the lap bars—and after a few years of fame it suddenly seemed to be out of synch with modern society's increasingly litigious mentality. The *Cyclone* was reworked repeatedly over the years as the park attempted to tame its inherent fury. Despite this, it's still a popular attraction at AstroWorld.

Other notable Bill Cobb-designed coasters which still operate much as their designer envisioned include the cover girl of this book, the spunky *Tornado* (1978, Des Moines, Iowa), the wild and wooly Riverside Park *Cyclone* (1983, Springfield, Massachusetts), the truly twisted *Le Monstre*—Cobb's only racing coaster

(1985, Montreal, Quebec), and the *Anaconda* in Metz, France.

John Pierce

Upon Bill Cobb's untimely death in 1990, his protege and assistant of 18 years, John Pierce, became an aggressive player in the field of wooden roller coaster design. Pierce had worked closely with Cobb on many of the above-mentioned projects and used the techniques and knowledge he had acquired to create several impressive thrillers of his own.

Aside from his input on the relocation and reprofiling of the dormant NAD-designed *Wildcat* from Kansas City's defunct Fairyland Park to Frontier City in Oklahoma City in 1991, he designed and consulted on a number of modern wooden coaster projects such as the *White Canyon* (another Coney Island *Cyclone* clone) at Yomiuri Land near Tokyo and *Twister II* at the new Elitch Gardens in Denver (1995), and the reassembling of the Crystal Beach *Comet* at New York's The Great Escape. But before he retired from the business, Pierce built a ride at San Antonio's Fiesta Texas that many enthusiasts agree had the best first drop of any wooden coaster they had ever ridden.

Called the *Rattler*, Pierce conjured up a radical design unlike anything the industry had witnessed. Opened in 1992, the *Rattler*'s protracted lift hill scaled the sheer rock wall of the abandoned quarry in which the new park was built. This towering 180-foot tall crest instantly broke the height record for a wooden roller coaster and put Fiesta Texas on the map. Though the *Rattler*'s highlights include a three-level helix atop the quarry, two swooping drops off the rim of the quarry wall, and a tunnel blasted through solid rock, the legendary first drop was the ride's crowning glory. At the time, this was the longest, steepest drop—166 feet—ever attempted on a wooden roller coaster. It was indeed magnificent and breathtaking, but this thriller's fame was to be short lived.

Interestingly, Pierce's *Rattler* suffered much of the same fate as did Cobb's original *Texas Cyclone*. A

JOHN PEIRCE AND HIS *RATTLER*

Funny, he *looks* like a regular sort of fellow, but John Pierce created a ride at Fiesta Texas near San Antonio that was deemed one of the most breathtaking and diabolical wood coasters ever. The credentials and dynamics of this massive twister had to be seen to be believed, and the first drop was its crowning glory. Upon release from the lift chain, trains slipped over the precipice, twisting first to the right and then to the left, all the while steepening to near vertical. The bottom of the first drop bottomed out sharply mere inches above the quarry floor and launched the train skyward over a hill and swooping back into the quarry. *Gary Slade*

THE *MEAN STREAK*

Curtis D. Summers had a "mean streak" in his mind, and it became reality at Cedar Point, Ohio. A mountain of dense wood structurework, the *Mean Streak* looms over all the other coasters at this coaster haven on the shores of Lake Erie. *Terry Lind*

few isolated rider complaints sensationalized by the media caught the attention of some attorneys. The resulting negative publicity influenced park management to reprofile this wonderful coaster, reducing it in both stature and thrills. The *Rattler*'s final and rather unorthodox indignation occurred when the bottom of its amazing first drop was raised 64 feet; it thus lost its record-breaking title. Those fans who experienced the *Rattler*'s original, mind-blowing first drop consider that sweet taste of true roller coaster glory a rare and auspicious event of their lives.

Since he worked behind the scenes for nearly two decades, John Pierce's contributions to the industry may not be as readily apparent as some of his colleagues. In any case, he will be forever remembered for the daring and creative energy he lavished on his projects, especially his incomparable *Rattler*.

The Dinn-Summers Amalgamation

Several other individuals and firms active during this period made an impact on the wooden coaster industry. Charles Dinn's name came to the forefront due to his involvement with the design and construction of the *Beast* at Kings Island in 1979. At 7,400 feet, it's still the world's longest wooden coaster and one that has become widely known by Midwesterners, if not folks from all over North America.

In 1985, Dinn supervised the relocation of the *Rocket*, a PTC wooden coaster standing dormant at a closed park in San Antonio, Texas, to Pennsylvania's Knoebel's Amusement Resort. That successful salvage project illustrated that moving existing wooden roller

coasters was not only possible but cost effective and beneficial in a number of other ways. Dinn and his crew subsequently moved and rebuilt two more classic rides that would have otherwise been lost forever: the *Giant Coaster* from Paragon Park at Hull, Massachusetts, to Maryland's Wild World (now Six Flags America), and the *Skyliner* from New York's Roseland Park to Pennsylvania's Lakemont Park. In addition, at Lake Compounce, Connecticut, Dinn rebuilt the *Wildcat* from the ground up in 1986.

With popularity in wooden roller coasters steadily increasing, Dinn teamed up with Curtis D. Summers, a talented engineer and designer who had assisted him on some of the relocation projects. Together—and usually under the name Curtis D. Summers Inc.—this energetic duo created popular rides like the *Raging Wolf Bobs* (built in 1988 at Geauga Lake near Cleveland, Ohio, and based loosely on the late lamented Riverview Park *Bobs*), *Timber Wolf* (1989, Kansas City), *Hercules* (1989, Allentown, Pennsylvania), *Texas Giant* (1990, Dallas/Fort Worth), the *Mean Streak* (1991, Sandusky, Ohio), and the highly rated *Georgia Cyclone* (built at Atlanta in 1990 and

continued on page 134

THE *WILD BEAST*

Based on the long-gone *Wildcat* coaster at Cincinnati's Coney Island, the *Wild Beast* at Canada's Wonderland was built by Curtis D. Summers Inc. and Taft Attractions, owner of the Toronto park. In this 1981 scene taken from on board the ride, a portion of the *Mighty Canadian Minebuster* is also visible, in the distance. The *Minebuster* is another Curtis D. Summers/Taft ride vaguely based on another vanished Coney Island coaster, the *Shooting Star. Mike Schafer*

THE *TEXAS GIANT*

Opened in 1990, Curtis Summers' mass of twisted lumber known as the *Texas Giant* featured a 143-foot lift hill—at the time the tallest of any wooden coaster—and a 4,920-foot run. The massive ride, with numerous unpredictable twists and turns and wide, swooping drops, has become a favorite of coaster fans everywhere. *Michael Bent*

Preserving the Past

The process of moving a structure as complex as a wooden roller coaster may seem an impossible task. True, it is not a simple thing to accomplish, but the feasibility of such an undertaking was clearly illustrated when Knoebel's Amusement Resort in Elysburg, Pennsylvania, purchased the 1947-built, Schmeck-designed *Rocket* from a defunct park in San Antonio, Texas. Under the direction Charles Dinn, the *Rocket* was carefully dismantled—its pieces painstakingly numbered—and transported to its new home in the scenic Pennsylvania woods.

Although a few wooden coasters had been moved in the past, the phenomenal and symbolic impact of the abandoned *Rocket* rising majestically as Knoebel's "new" *Phoenix* cannot be overestimated.

In the same vein of historical preservation are a few very significant wooden roller coasters that had been closed and faced almost certain extinction, but at the Eleventh Hour were saved, revamped, and reopened at their original locations. There is a certain poetic justice in rehabilitating a dormant coaster in its native environment.

Two such prominent preservation projects that must be noted are the *Giant Dipper* in San Diego, California, and *Leap The Dips* at Lakemont Park in Altoona, Pennsylvania. Though very different rides, these two influential examples of roller coaster engineering are direct links to the amusement industry's heritage. They both deserve to remain intact and operational as monuments to a proud and glorious past.

Leap The Dips

The more recent of these two rides to reopen was *Leap The Dips*, currently the world's oldest operating roller coaster, originally built in 1902. It is also the only remaining example of the ultra-popular figure-8 coasters, hundreds of which populated amusement parks worldwide at the dawn of the twentieth century. With the arrival of

THE *PHOENIX*

Though not a particularly large ride by today's standards, the *Phoenix* delivers a rip-roarin' ride that has put this coaster on many current Top Ten lists. This 1985 view looks down the *Phoenix*'s first hill and elongated figure-8 track arrangement. *Mike Schafer*

LEAP-THE-DIPS

Modern-day riders enjoy a near-century-old ride in 1999 following the rededication of Lakemont Park's elderly *Leap-the-Dips* Figure-8 coaster. *Mark Davidson*

faster and more extreme rides following World War I, these gentle rides suddenly became obsolete and nearly all of them vanished.

Amazingly, Lakemont Park's *Leap The Dips* managed to survive and remain in operation for over 80 years, but in 1985, Lakemont Park closed the old ride but left it intact. A contingent of concerned citizens and coaster fans, notably the American Coaster Enthusiasts, tirelessly worked to have *Leap The Dips* placed on the National Register of Historic Places, which happened in March 1991; though not operational, it received National Landmark Status in June 1996.

The *Leap The Dips* Preservation Foundation, Inc.—a not-for-profit volunteer group—was established in 1994 for the purpose of raising the funds necessary to restore, operate, maintain, and preserve *Leap The Dips*. The ride was officially returned to service on Memorial Day 1999. With great fanfare, the first passengers boarded the four-passenger cars to embark on the very same adventure their ancestors had nearly a century earlier.

Giant Dipper, San Diego, California

Another important act of historical preservation mirrors the *Leap The Dips* saga to some extent, though instead of having at least the support of a surrounding park, this one was a stand alone derelict that cheated the hangman a number of times before being rescued.

Opened July 4, 1925, the *Giant Dipper* at Belmont Park in San Diego was a unique example of Fred Church's *Bobs* coasters. For 51 years, the *Giant Dipper* was the star of Belmont Park. But in 1976, the park closed and the *Giant Dipper* (by then having been renamed *Earthquake*) fell silent. Interestingly, the coaster appeared as a backdrop for an episode of the 1970s TV drama series "Family" in which actress (and coaster fan) Kristy McNichol ran away from her Pasadena home to San Diego.

Coaster enthusiasts and native residents who had grown up with the ride were disheartened to see such a classic example of roller coaster craftsmanship being left to rot. A grass-roots movement—the Save the Coaster Committee—was formed to bring attention to the plight of the *Giant Dipper*. The ride was declared a National Historic Landmark and the San Diego Seaside Company set about restoring the *Giant Dipper*.

The reconstruction process adhered closely to Fred Church's

SAN DIEGO'S *GIANT DIPPER*

The colorful *Giant Dipper* at San Diego's Belmont Park takes another trainload of guests for a tour of Fred Church's signature drops and turns. *Terry Lind*

original 1925 design. On August 11, 1990, the venerable *Giant Dipper* was returned to service. The new Morgan Manufacturing trains, donated by Morgan for the cause, plied the twisted course with an elegant grace not seen for far too long. Paying customers flocked in droves to have a whirl aboard this genuine classic and made it far more profitable than anyone would have hoped.

Today, the *Giant Dipper* is as popular as ever, reigning majestically over Mission Beach as it did for generations. Thanks to the valorous efforts of those who fought the good fight in the name of preservation, the sweet melody of a vintage seaside twister once again competes with the Pacific's timeless roar.

IDAHO'S COASTERS

Custom Coasters International has thus far built two coasters for Silverwood Theme Park in Athol, Idaho: the *Timber Terror* and *Tremors*. The former is a classic out-and-back design complete with a rugged helix and loads of CCI's trademark airtime. The latter ride is a surprising gem of coaster due to its four underground tunnels. One of these subterranean caves exits through the floor of a gift shop, violently rattling the building to its very foundation. *Otto P. Dobnick.*

continued from page 131

yet another spin on the ever-popular Coney Island *Cyclone*). All examples of this fruitful collaboration.

DENISE DINN

Following in the footsteps of her father, Charles Dinn (the *Beast*, Kings Island), Denise Dinn has made coasters her career. She is owner of Custom Coasters International. *Gary Slade*

Custom Coasters International

Custom Coasters of West Chester, Ohio, is a spirited firm that vigorously excels in the art of wooden roller coaster construction. Owned by Denise Dinn-Larrick, daughter of coaster builder Charles Dinn, CCI is without question the most prolific wooden coaster company around today, and their products have been met with high praise.

Dinn-Larrick began working with her father back when his own company was just gathering steam. Over the years, she worked on numerous coaster relocations as well as brand new rides, accumulating detailed knowledge about materials, blueprints, and trade terms. Learning the business from the inside out gave her a realistic view of what this intensely specialized craft is all about. When Charles Dinn retired,

SHIVERING TIMBERS

A monumental mass of wood, Custom Coasters International's *Shivering Timbers* at Michigan's Adventure near Muskegon is the most awesome out-and-back coaster of the renaissance age. Its numerous deep, deep dips pay tribute to John Miller rides of the 1920s. When the 125-foot tall coaster opened in 1998, it shot to a prominent spot on many enthusiasts' Top Ten lists. Sources confirm that park owners are scouting a location for their fourth woodie. *Mike Schafer*

Denise decided to carry on the family tradition and open her own company. Accompanied by husband Randy Larrick, brother Jeff Dinn, her father as consultant, and crack team of designers, engineers, and builders, CCI has emerged as a dynamic force in the amusement industry.

With sparkling original designs bearing a taste of the Roaring Twenties, many of CCI's creations offer downright amazing amounts of airtime and intense lateral G forces. The maverick design techniques employed by CCI virtually guarantee that their rides will be enormously popular with the general public. Of course, hard-core coaster fans flock to CCI coasters due the company's reputation of building no-holds barred, wild, and intense thrillers.

Custom Coasters' design team obviously takes great pleasure in what it does. Multiple CCI crews can be found at any given time working on projects around the world. They've built more than 25 rides over the past nine years, among them the *Hoosier Hurricane* (1991, Indiana Beach, Monticello, Indiana), *Outlaw* (1993, Adventureland, Des Moines, Iowa), the *Raven* (1995, Holiday World, Santa Claus, Indiana); the *Great White* (1995, Wild Wheels Pier, Wildwood, New Jersey); a trio of wonderful woodies—the *Cyclops* (1995), *Pegasus* (1996), and *Zeus* (1997)—at Big Chief Kart and Coaster Park, Wisconsin Dells; the *Rampage* (1998, Birmingham, Alabama), and—quite possibly CCI's ultimate—*Shivering Timbers* (1998, Michigan's Adventure, Muskegon). The company has a bounty of thrillers on tap for the new Millennium.

Great Coasters International

Although Custom Coasters may be the busiest of the new wooden coaster builders, Great Coasters International, based in Sunbury, Pennsylvania, and Santa Cruz, California, has a noble mission of creating "retro-classical" coasters. Co-owners Michael Boodley (designer) and Clair Hain Jr. (builder) are obviously influenced by the likes of John Miller, Harry Traver, and the Vettle family. But it's because of Boodley's and Hain's obvious admiration of the unparalleled

Fred Church that their projects take on a graceful, well-defined uniqueness.

Mike Boodley reminisces how, as a boy growing up in New Jersey, he wanted to design wooden roller coasters. At 17, his passion for these rides found him at New York's Coney Island where he set a coaster endurance record by completing 1,001 laps on the legendary *Cyclone*. His education carried him into the field of mechanical and structural engineering, and he bided his time by perfecting his skills until he was ready to pursue his dream. His natural love and enthusiasm for the golden age legends continually shows up in his designs.

Though Boodley and Hain each worked for other coaster builders prior to launching their own business, their first project under the GCI banner was the *Wildcat* at Pennsylvania's Hersheypark. Opened in 1996, this delightful ride, like most GCI coasters, depicts the golden age twister layout in every sense of the word.

Next came *Roar* in 1998 at Six Flags America near Washington, D.C., followed by 1999's *Gwazi* at Busch Gardens Tampa Bay. This gargantuan double-tracked "dueling coaster" is simply amazing. It features numerous instances where the opposing trains encounter each other during near-miss flybys at a combined speed of over 100 MPH.

But it was out in Vallejo, California, in the Spring of 1999 that GCI really brought the past back to life. Boodley and Hain borrowed the *Roar* footprint from Six Flags America, jazzed it up, tweaked it, and made it a little more rambunctious than its Eastern cousin. Besides building an outstanding example of a golden age twister, it was on this ride—also named *Roar*—that GCI unveiled its exclusive new single-seat articulated rolling stock.

Affectionately dubbed Millennium Flyers (a clever nod to NAD's wonderful old deco-inspired Century Flyers), these 14-car, ultra-flexible trains sport rare open fronts and flared sides like those from the Prior & Church mold. Coupled with *Roar*'s tangled track plan, the retro look and feel of these sleek trains made it seem as if

continued on page 142

GCI'S MICHAEL BOODLEY AND CLAIR HAIN JR.

Partners Michael Boodley (left) and Clair Hain Jr. operated Great Coasters International. *Gary Slade*

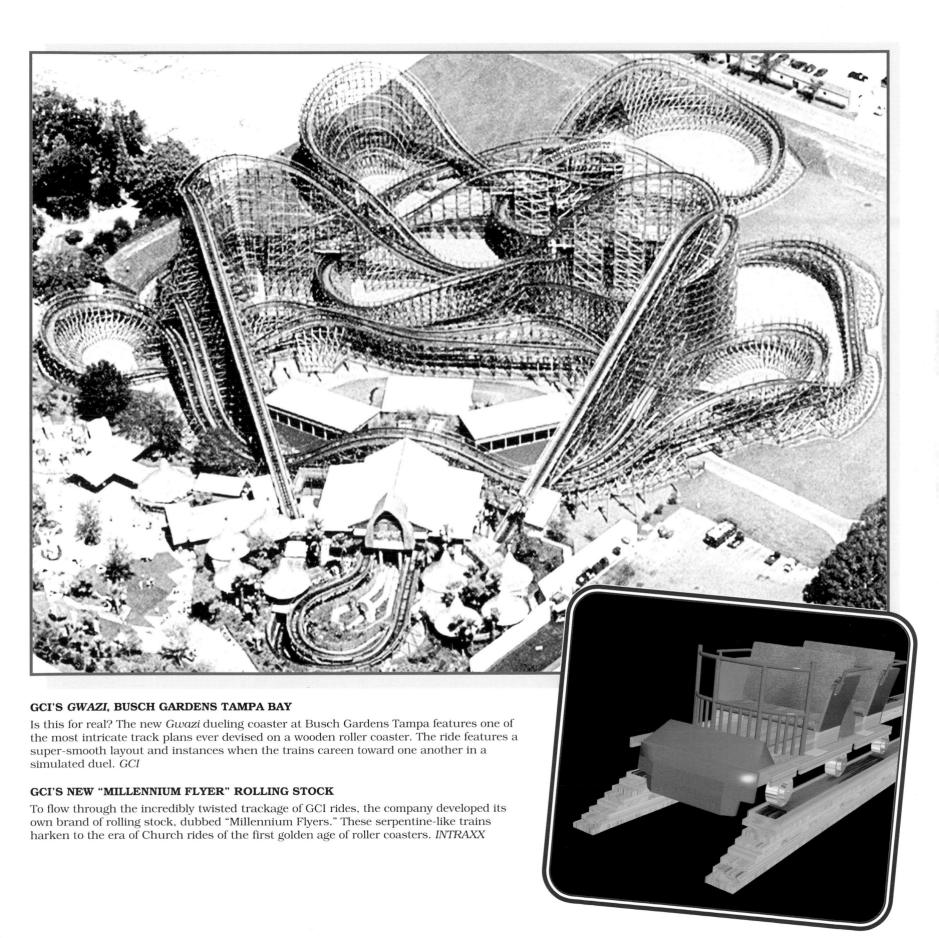

GCI'S *GWAZI*, BUSCH GARDENS TAMPA BAY

Is this for real? The new *Gwazi* dueling coaster at Busch Gardens Tampa features one of the most intricate track plans ever devised on a wooden roller coaster. The ride features a super-smooth layout and instances when the trains careen toward one another in a simulated duel. *GCI*

GCI'S NEW "MILLENNIUM FLYER" ROLLING STOCK

To flow through the incredibly twisted trackage of GCI rides, the company developed its own brand of rolling stock, dubbed "Millennium Flyers." These serpentine-like trains harken to the era of Church rides of the first golden age of roller coasters. *INTRAXX*

Renaissance Classics

Now that the amusement industry and the roller coaster bask in the radiance of the second golden age, a number of exceptional rides built during the initial stages of this renaissance stand out as ground-breakers, superstars in a galaxy of stellar thrillers. Here is a selection of high-profile installations that all have, in their own way, made an impact on the industry and the public alike and are likely to be considered classics for years to come.

The Racer, Paramount's Kings Island, Cincinnati, Ohio

As previously mentioned, the debut of the Racer in 1972 was an extraordinarily important event directly linked to the resurgence of interest in the roller coaster. John Allen of the Philadelphia Toboggan Company designed this mirror-image racing coaster to be not only an entertaining ride but a thing of structural beauty and elegance. The view from the top of the 88-foot lift hill is rather awe inspiring: The twin wooden tracks split gracefully near the ride's distant turnaround, swing around in opposite directions, and then converge for a spirited jaunt back to the station.

Kings Island gave the *Racer* an added twist in 1982 by turning the trains around backward on one track without changing the direction of travel. This provided riders with a brand-new (and disorienting) perspective. Several other parks around the country followed Kings Island's lead and have reversed trains on their own rides.

Texas Cyclone, Six Flags AstroWorld, Houston

The *Texas Cyclone*, which opened at Houston's AstroWorld in 1976 (prior to the park's becoming a Six Flags property), was the first wooden coaster project tackled by Bill Cobb and his design team. At the time, the "T-Clone's" inspiration—the original Coney

THE *TEXAS CYCLONE*

Bigger, badder, and many would say better than its New York protege, the *Texas Cyclone* is one of the classics of the new golden era of roller coasters. Drastic reprofiling over the years has tamed the ride. *Mike Schafer*

Island *Cyclone*—was in imminent danger of being dismantled. AstroWorld officials even considered moving it to Texas. After Cobb completed an evaluation of the New York ride, it was deemed that a modified version of the Coney classic was a more feasible option. Cobb was told to design an improved, Texas-sized version of the original *Cyclone*.

Cobb took those vague words of guidance quite literally, and the resulting ride seemed to have materialized right out of the first golden age. This radical coaster was a mirror-image re-creation of the Coney *Cyclone*, though in many ways a superior ride.

Taller and faster than its big-city cousin, the *Texas Cyclone* became an instant world-class twister that demanded respect and submission from its riders. Coaster fans immediately ranked it as the world's new No. 1 woodie. Abrupt break-overs, savage, slamming turns, and devilish negative Gs made the *Texas Cyclone* a force to be reckoned with.

Unfortunately, today's *Texas Cyclone* is a far different ride than the one Cobb originally envisioned and constructed. America's lawsuit-minded society and the current industry atmosphere simply are not conducive to the unbridled nature of the original *Texas Cyclone*. Beginning a few seasons after its celebrated debut, the ride was subjected to a battery of mysterious alterations. It has been reworked, cut down, re-profiled, and tamed to the point where it is a far cry from the aggressive thriller that so many celebrated. The ride's current, newer fiberglass rolling stock is equipped with vision-impeding headrests that surround the rider and detract greatly from the overall experience. Many fans fortunate enough to have ridden the *Texas Cyclone* in its heyday still agree that no operating wooden coaster can match the sheer intensity this ride had when it opened in 1976.

The Beast, Paramount's Kings Island, Cincinnati, Ohio

When this wooden behemoth opened in 1979, the public and the industry were justifiably astonished. Like the *Titanic*, the audacious scale of the *Beast* was mind-boggling. With 7,400 feet of track, the ride became the world's longest wooden roller coaster. Even today that notable record remains intact.

Designed and built in-house under the direction of Charles Dinn, this enormous terrain-driven monster covers an amazing 35 acres of forested real estate. Perhaps what makes the *Beast* even more enigmatic—and even a bit frightening, especially at night—is the fact that it was purposely built away from the main area of the

THE *BEAST*, KINGS ISLAND, CINCINNATI, OHIO

Consistently rated as one of the best roller coasters in North America, the *Beast* is a coaster legend. One of the few wooden coasters in the world to feature two lift hills, the *Beast* likewise has split personalities: In one sense it's a traditional roller coaster with one of the better first drops (into *The Tunnel That Is Too Small For The Coaster Trains*), a giant runaway mine train, and a terrifying animal trying to shake those riders from its back. In this view from early in the *Beast*'s career, we're looking over the shoulders of riders about to experience the first drop (note the tunnel entrance) while a second train has just disengaged from the second lift hill in the distance. The terrifying "Beast's Lair"—the roofed helix (before it was completely enclosed, as it is today)—is fully visible at right in all its vicious glory. *Kings Island* park. From no vantage point (other than an aircraft) can the complete layout be viewed. This clever concealment heightens the thrill, since riders really have no idea what to expect as they go tearing blindly through the woods.

The *Beast*'s first hill drops 135 feet directly into a noisy, underground concrete tunnel. A curving pull-out flings riders over an embankment and into a series of wide swooping turns, shallow hills, and another long tunnel. All the while, the lengthy six-car train's velocity increases. If you are fortunate to ride with the *Beast* when it is in top form (after a rainstorm or at night when the ride has been running all day and a light dew has settled on the tracks), you'll swear the rocketing trains are trying to rip free of their wooden bonds.

Two thirds of the way through the course, riders are granted a brief reprieve—a rare second chain lift. As the train climbs high above the trees, vigilant riders might catch a glimpse of another loaded train cresting the first hill to head into what they just experienced. Before they have time to watch their neighbors, their own train careens down a 141-foot speed ramp into what is arguably one of the most outrageous finales in coaster history: a 540-degree tunneled helix negotiated at unfathomable pace. This dark, jarring whirlwind of screeching steel-on-steel madness leaves riders shaken and stirred, yet exuberant.

The Revolution, Six Flags Magic Mountain, Valencia, California

This beautiful machine was opened in 1976 at Magic Mountain before Six Flags arrived on the scene. A product of Anton Schwarzkopf and Intamin, it was the first modern steel roller coaster to successfully send riders through a vertical loop. Though that single inversion was the main attention grabber, the overall package was a striking image of graceful lines rendered in white steel.

The *Revolution*, immediately hailed as an engineering masterpiece, is seamlessly integrated into the park's rugged hills and ravines. During the 3,457-foot-long ride, some of the drops catch riders off guard because they are longer and more pronounced than a casual perusal of the visible track layout reveals.

The *Revolution* became an international star when it took top billing in the Universal movie *Rollercoaster* in 1977. Today, the *Revolution* has been tamed by heavy braking and a restrictive, unnecessary over-the-shoulder restraint system, yet it is still an interesting ride deserving of recognition.

THE *REVOLUTION*, SIX FLAGS MAGIC MOUNTAIN

The first modern looping coaster, the *Revolution* took top billing in the 1977 feature film, *Rollercoaster*. For many years this beautiful, sprawling ride was one of the best steel coasters around. Cumbersome over-the-shoulder harnesses and excessive braking have nudged it down a few notches. *Otto P. Dobnick*

Riverside Cyclone, Riverside Park, Agawam (Springfield), Massachusetts

When designer Bill Cobb was asked to design a wild wooden coaster for Riverside's 1983 season, he jumped at the chance, despite the fact that he was in the hospital for heart surgery. As it turned out, there was very little available land on which to place his new *Cyclone*, and he was forced to devise a tight, interwoven layout. True to his genius (or madness, depending on one's point of view), the resulting thriller was a ride unlike any other modern coaster.

Often considered one of the most ferocious woodies in operation today, the *Cyclone* grabs riders by the throat with a diabolical, one-of-kind twisted double-dip maneuver. A steep dive from 107 feet in the air leads into a severe right turn halfway down, followed by a slight rise as the train rolls onto its side and then screams toward the ground. The remainder of this compressed, 3,400-foot-long twister is loaded with violent direction changes, fierce drops, and other hidden surprises. Unlike Cobb's *Texas Cyclone*, the Riverside *Cyclone* has not suffered from extreme re-profiling. It is still pretty much the same intense, untamed experience Cobb envisioned. Though considered brutal by some standards, this *Cyclone* is very popular with park guests and coaster enthusiasts alike.

Mindbenders, West Edmonton and Six Flags over Georgia

Though these two steel loopers share the same name and designer, each offers unique features that earn them places of honor as influential rides.

The *Mindbender* at Six Flags Over Georgia is often mistakenly referred to as the world's first triple-loop steel coaster. Custom-designed by Anton Schwarzkopf in 1978, the *Mindbender* sits on the edge of a deep ravine at the front of the park. Graceful turns, two vertical loops, long drops, and a heavily banked mid-course swoop into the ravine (the misnamed third loop) all combine to make this ride a favorite. It also earns bonus points for rider freedom: The *Mindbender* is one of the few remaining major loopers that does not utilize an over-the-shoulder restraint system.

And then there's the other *Mindbender*, the wicked Canadian stepsister. Built in 1983, this intimidating ride rules the cavernous confines of Canada's West Edmonton Mall (Edmonton, Alberta).

Those wanting a real taste of extreme coastering should make the long trek north; the *Mindbender* is really that good. Schwarzkopf basically took the footprint of his *Dreier Looping* (a triple looper built for the German fair circuit) and enlarged it to the point where it nearly scrapes the mall's soaring ceiling. This 13-story ride features fiendishly steep suicide plunges from the rafters, twisted climbs, and three vertical loops, which all guarantee near-blackout positive G forces. The *Mindbender* utilizes a very short three-car train arrangement which translates into little or no push-pull effect and sustained, blinding speed along the 4,080 feet of track. This is one steel coaster most definitely not for the timid.

***MAGNUM XL200*, CEDAR POINT, SANDUSKY, OHIO**

When *Magnum* opened in 1989, the world was stunned by this first hypercoaster's 205-foot lift hill, 60-degree first drop, and ride intensity. More than a decade later, the excellent ride still rates as one of the most popular steel roller coasters on the planet, hyper or otherwise. *David P. Oroszi*

Magnum XL200, Cedar Point, Sandusky, Ohio

A spin aboard *Magnum* is an unforgettable, almost spiritual roller coaster experience, not simply because it was the first hypercoaster, but because it is truly awe-inspiring. Maybe it's the sense of exposure: The ride is perched right on the beach, inches from the lapping waves of Lake Erie. The view itself is worth the trip. Or maybe it's because *Magnum* is located in one of the most incredible amusement parks in the world—13 coasters as this book went to press. Whatever the case, this steel giant takes riders to unfathomed levels in thrills.

With a lift height of 205 feet and a 195-foot first drop angled at an amazingly steep 60 degrees, "breathtaking" hardly comes close to describing the sensation of *Magnum*'s opening act. Each succeeding hill offers something unique, whether it's encased in a tight tunnel loaded with special light, sound, and fog effects, or shaped to produce dramatic (and often abrupt) degrees of sustained airtime. Even though bigger and faster coasters are already in operation, *Magnum* will always hold a special place in the hearts of those who love a coaster with staying power. Regardless of how many times you've ridden it, *Magnum XL200* is one of those rare ride experiences that remains with you long after you hit the home brakes.

continued from page 136

the whole machine had been plucked straight out of the 1920s.

GCI's initial twenty-first-century project is the world's first racing/dueling coaster. Joining their very own *Wildcat* at Hersheypark, the new ride sports the intriguing name of *Lightning Racer* and promises to be one heck of an experience. Four GCI Millennium Flyers will subject riders to a furious tour of complex trackage, sometimes racing side by side, then splitting away to arc through tight turns which will lead them into a face-to-face dueling situation.

Of course, customers have come to expect such ingenuity and attention to detail from the fellows at Great Coasters. Their rides are painstakingly crafted to be visually engaging as well as structurally functional. GCI builds with an elegance and finesse not seen seen for decades.

Renaissance Designers and Firms: Steel-Track Coaster

Anton Schwarzkopf, Herr Achterbahn

On the steel coaster front, there are several individuals and firms that embraced steel roller coaster technology from its infancy at mid-century on, and they remained dedicated to steel coasters into the second golden age.

As mentioned in chapter 4, Arrow Development's Carl Bacon, Ed Morgan, and, later, Ron Toomer pioneered steel roller coaster technology in the U.S. during the post-World War II years through their advancements with the unique concept of tubular rails and nylon or polyurethane wheels.

At the same time, a German named Anton Schwarzkopf, reared near Munich, had several of his own ideas on the subject of steel coasters. Today the name Schwarzkopf is synonymous with quality amusement-ride construction, especially steel roller coasters, both portable and permanent.

Schwarzkopf designed his first steel coaster, the *Wildcat*, in 1964. This non-looping, figure-eight style ride featured single four-passenger vehicles zipping down steep drops and swirling spirals. Though it employed flat rails like those found on smaller *Wild Mouse*-type coasters, the *Wildcat* was much

smoother and more quiet due to its wheels being made of a durable polyurethane-like compound.

By 1968, Schwarzkopf had switched to the tubular rail format, and that's when the real fun began. First came the *Jet Stars*—compact high-speed tubular-rail coasters sporting severely banked turns and abrupt, though smooth, transitions. They were all the rage. Progressively larger versions, both portable and park models, came out of Schwarzkopf's Munsterhausen factory and found homes all over the globe.

With each new roller coaster concept that Schwarzkopf and his team rolled out, they always surprised industry watchers with their inventiveness. The company made many contributions to amusement ride technology, especially with pipe bending techniques. The company's unique "cone-and-plug" construction system made the assembly of these amazing rides—especially the transportable versions—incredibly efficient and manageable.

Beginning in 1971, a series of permanent park coasters generically referred to as Speedracers came

next. At Six Flags Over Texas, the Speedracer *Big Bend* opened to glowing reviews followed by *Willard's Whizzers* at both Great Americas (California and Illinois) and the near-twin *Zambezi Zinger* at Worlds of Fun at Kansas City, Missouri.

Then, as outlined earlier in this chapter, Schwarzkopf in 1976 threw everyone for a loop—a vertical loop, on the new *Revolution* at California's Magic Mountain theme park. Larger and loopier

ANTON SCHWARZKOPF

This nattily attired German was the king of steel coastering in Europe, and his work is also praised by countless park-goers in North America and around the world. Herr Schwarzkopf is shown on the brake run of what he cited as his favorite coaster, the *Lisebergbahn* at Liseberg Park, Gothenburg, Sweden. This sweeping non-looping steel coaster is built into a densely wooded hillside and displays the Master's creative hand at designing a speedy, pleasant ride and integrating it seamlessly into the surrounding environment. *Markus Marbach/European Coaster Club*

WILLARD'S WHIZZER

Basically an outgrowth of the portable *Jumbo Jet* rides found throughout the U.S., *Willard's Whizzer*, *Big Bend*, and *Zambezi Zinger* make for good "starter" rides for up-and-coming coaster enthusiasts. This is the *Whizzer* at Great America at San Jose, California, in 1987 as viewed from the lift helix. *Otto P. Dobnick*

SCHWARZKOPF'S *THRILLER*

Schwarzkopf has produced a series of compact—yet intense—portable coasters that are enormously popular in Europe and elsewhere. Many coaster connoisseurs feel that Schwarzkopf's masterpiece is the *Thriller*. The ride is shown at Six Flags AstroWorld, Houston, Texas, in its new incarnation as *Taz's Texas Tornado*. Typical of Schwarzkopf rides, this convoluted mass of trackage delivers a sensuous, flowing, yet ultra dynamic ride experience. *Gary Slade*

TRAINS BY MORGAN MANUFACTURING

Dana Morgan's company is best known for the construction of rolling stock, both for new rides such as the Riverside *Cyclone* and older rides, such as the *Giant Dipper* at Belmont Park, San Diego. In this 1990 scene at Seabreeze Park near Rochester, New York, a shiny new Morgan train hops through the course of the *Jack Rabbit*, a 1920 Miller & Baker ride famous for its surprise ending. *Mike Schafer*

RON TOOMER

Ron Toomer is a key designer in the world of tubular steel coasters. *Gary Slade*

examples followed at parks around the world as well as portable versions for traveling fairs.

Some of Schwarzkopf's most famous rides include the *Sooperdooperlooper* (1977, Hersheypark, Hershey, Pennsylvania), the *Mindbender*s at Six Flags Over Georgia and Canada's West Edmonton (Alberta) Mall (1978 and 1986 respectively), and the *Shockwave* (1978, Six Flags Over Texas). Several Schwarzkopf/Intamin shuttle loops with vertical reverse points operate at parks around the world. As for traveling rides, there are many, but one model in particular stands out: the *Thriller*. One serves as a permanent installation at Six Flags AstroWorld in Texas where it is known as the *Taz Texas Tornado*.

Anton Schwarzkopf's exemplary career is a shining example of vivid imagination combined with passion and determination. Though the master designer

retired in 1995 to his native Germany, his brilliant steel roller coasters are still going strong. In fact, the demand for the Schwarzkopf product is so great today that Anton's son, Wieland, is offering original designs to new clients. It appears that the Schwarzkopf legacy will live on well into the twenty-first century. And that seems entirely appropriate since Anton always was ahead of his time.

Ron Toomer

Ron Toomer came to the industry in 1965 when he was hired by Arrow trendsetters Ed Morgan and Carl Bacon as a mechanical engineer to assist in the creation of the first *Runaway Mine Train* at Six Flags Over

Texas. He went on to assist in the development of a number of ground-breaking coasters, including the first *Corkscrew* at Knott's Berry Farm in 1975.

Arrow ownership changed hands until eventually becoming today's Arrow Dynamics. During his long tenure with the company, Toomer contributed to the evolution of the steel roller coaster from the relatively simple *Corkscrew* to a vast assortment of complex installations. Some of Toomer's more notable steel coasters include the *Loch Ness Monster* (1978, Busch Gardens, Virginia), the *Orient Express* (1980, Worlds of Fun, Kansas City), the *Big Bad Wolf* (1984, also Busch Gardens), and the stellar *Magnum XL200* (1989, Cedar Point). Having since left Arrow, he is at work on a number of independent projects.

Dana H. Morgan

Dana Morgan literally grew up in the business. The son of coaster pioneer Ed Morgan, he watched his dad work on Disneyland's *Matterhorn Bobsleds* and was the first child ever to ride the *Bobsleds* prototype at the Arrow factory. He grew to love the industry and went on to work in an engineering capacity for the Disney organization and eventually with his father at Arrow.

After a stint as general manager of the Santa Cruz Beach and Boardwalk—home of the exquisite 1924-built *Giant Dipper* wooden twister—Morgan was appointed president of the short-live Arrow/Huss amalgamation and then opened his own company, D. H. Morgan Manufacturing. Morgan's new company was known primarily for its classic carousels, but quickly moved into building trains for wood coasters.

The firm really leaped into the limelight with a string of 200-plus-foot tall non-looping "hypercoasters" (next chapter) such as the *Steel Force* (1997, Allentown, Pennsylvania), *Mamba* (1998, Kansas City) and the *Steel Eel* (1999, World of Texas).

Intamin AG

Intamin (an acronym for INTernational AMusement INstallation) is another ride builder whose name has been associated with a wide variety of designers and manufacturers. Originally based in Zurich, Switzerland, this renowned firm began by building observation towers, cableways and transportation systems for parks and resorts. It jumped onto the roller coaster bandwagon and is now major force in this sector of the industry.

Vekoma

Vekoma International of the Netherlands has been around for many years. Beside a series of standard looping and family-style steel coasters, the company's first major hit was the *Boomerang* shuttle loop. This off-the-shelf model has appeared in parks the world over. A more recent entry, and one that has proved just as popular, is an exciting suspended looping

coaster. Like the *Boomerang*, this intense thriller is a popular choice for parks looking for high-profile, yet compact thrillers to add to their coaster collections.

Various

Space doesn't allow us to list each steel coaster manufacturer, but other notable firms include Giovanola (Switzerland), Pinfari (Italy), Zamperla (Italy), Mack (Germany), Mauer Sohne (Germany), Zierer (Germany), Reverchon (France), the Miler Coaster Company, and O. D. Hopkins (both U.S.).

VEKOMA *BOOMERANG*
Vekoma took the standard shuttle-loop concept of a single loop and twisted it into a loop, a boomerang element, and a track that folded back onto itself. This *Boomerang* thrills riders forward and backward at Knott's Berry Farm. *Terry Lind*

New Age Coastering

Now and Beyond

Technology has vastly altered life as we know it on this planet. One can look at it as an invasion into the realm of "it's just fine the way it is, thank you!" or as a launching pad for new opportunities and experiences. And this includes the world of roller coasters, too. There are a tremendous number of coaster enthusiasts out there who simply prefer the joys of a John Miller wooden classic built in 1927. Oh, they may sample the new-age coaster that just opened next to the venerable woodie, but afterwards they'll head back to their tried-and-proven friend from the Roaring Twenties.

DESERT STORMING

A packed *Desperado* train plummets down the 225-foot first drop at Buffalo Bill's south of Las Vegas, Nevada. Opened in 1994, this Arrow Dynamics hypercoaster held the North American record for biggest drop (tied with Kennywood Park's *Steel Phantom*) until 2000. Riders board *Desperado* inside the casino and are then hoisted up the lift through an opening in the roof. After the initial 80-MPH plunge into an underground tunnel, the train blasts though a series of banked turns, wild negative-G hops and other surprises. *Desperado* is of the West's wildest rides. *Scott Rutherford*

HYPER INTENSITY

Unveiled in 1989, *Magnum XL200* at Cedar Point in Sandusky, Ohio, was the world's very first hypercoaster. Its picturesque location on a sandy beach mere inches from Lake Erie offers an awe-inspiring view during the clanking trip to the top of the 205-foot lift hill. Of course, that's all forgotten once the train slips into its 60-degree power dive. Sustained airtime, a rollicking pretzel turnaround, and several tunnels make the *Magnum* experience truly unforgettable. *Scott Rutherford*

On the other hand, there are those aficionados who simply love coaster thrills any way they can get it: wood or steel; chain-driven lift hills or linear-induction catapults; up-and-down camelback humps or mind-numbing loops, boomerangs, and other countless inversions.

Hypercoastering: Scaling New Heights

In 1989, Arrow Dynamics rocked the amusement industry by being the first ride manufacturer to achieve the elusive 200-foot height mark for a continuous circuit roller coaster. Called *Magnum XL200*, this groundbreaking steel thriller debuted at Cedar Point in Sandusky, Ohio. It earned the title of the world's very first "hypercoaster," a term coined to designate a coaster standing 200 feet or taller. Though it was fashioned completely of steel—tubular rails atop a galvanized metal support structure—it had no loops and mimicked the traditional up-and-down motion of the classic out-and-back wooden coaster. It was an instant success. (See the "Renaissance Classics" sidebar in chapter 5 for a description of the ride.)

Arrow Dynamics and rival steel-coaster builder Morgan Manufacturing introduced several more hypercoasters over the next few years. Each is an entertaining ride in many respects, but two stand out: Arrow's *Desperado* at Buffalo Bill's near Las Vegas, Nevada, and the looping *Steel Phantom* at Pittsburgh's Kennywood Park attained the record for North America's tallest coaster drops: 225 feet.

Desperado isn't at a park, but is part of a hotel and casino complex at Primm, Nevada. In fact, *Desperado's* loading station is in a casino! Trains engage the lift hill and then exit the building through a opening in the roof. The lift hill crests at 209 feet, but—using a trick pioneered by Chicago's Riverview Park which had to circumvent city covenants limiting the height of a coaster—the first drop tunnels underground to

achieve its record drop of 225 feet. Beyond are classic hills—some with outrageous negative Gs—and swoop turns as coaster trains roar past parking areas and building fronts. The mile-long-plus ride concludes with an enclosed upward spiral.

Kennywood's *Steel Phantom* accomplishes its 225-foot drop in a similar way, as the lift hill stands "only" 160 feet high, towering over the park's nearby coaster star, the *Thunderbolt*, with its 70-foot lift hill. The *Steel Phantom's* second drop is its record-breaker, diving 225 feet down *through* the structure of the old *Pippin* section of the *Thunderbolt* (actually *under* the bottom of the *Thunderbolt's* second drop)

and over the bluff. The pullout is on a ledge partway down the bluff, and it sends trains back up to the main level of the park where they go through the usual set of inversions found on today's steelies: vertical loops, barrel rolls, and such, some of them causing near-blackout condition for some riders.

New Age Inversions

In 1990, a new firm called Bollinger & Mabillard based in Monthey, Switzerland, appeared on the scene and breathed new life into the industry with a second-generation standup coaster. This ride, called the *Iron Wolf*, was built at Six Flags Great America

KUMBA

Busch Gardens Tampa Bay was the first customer to receive Bollinger & Mabillard's sitdown looping coaster. Opened in 1993, *Kumba* was an instant hit. Perhaps it has something to do with a B&M coaster's trademark smoothness and rideability. Three eight-car trains (riders sit four-abreast per vehicle) are subjected to a whirlwind tour of the 3,978-foot long course. *Kumba's* 135-foot first drop is followed by a huge vertical loop encircling the lift hill, and six more disorienting inversions. The ride's underground tunnel finale is a scream! *Busch Gardens*

BATMAN—THE RIDE

B&M rocked the amusement industry when it introduced the inverted-coaster concept at Six Flags Great America (Chicago) in 1992. *Batman—The Ride* features a swooping 10-story first drop followed by two vertical loops, a zero-G heartline spin, and a pair of intense corkscrews. With 2,693 feet of twisted trackage, *Batman* (like most other B&M coasters) executes its transitions with unparalleled grace and fluidity. This particular layout proved so popular that B&M delivered clones for five more Six Flags theme parks in the U.S., in addition to copies erected at several other parks around the world. *Terry Lind*

and featured a complex layout packed with severe banking and multiple inversions. What really caught everyone's attention, though, was the precise engineering techniques employed in B&M's debut effort. This stringent attention to detail made the *Iron Wolf* unbelievably smooth despite the wild gyrations it was performing. This superb coaster also featured a four-across seating configuration, a trait that would consistently show up on nearly all B&M coasters.

Several other notable B&M stand-ups materialized at U.S. theme parks, including rides at Paramount's Great America and Paramount's Carowinds. As it turned out, these glass-smooth crowd pleasers were but a preview of what B&M had up its sleeve.

In 1992, while other manufacturers were churning out relatively normal looping coaster installations, B&M unveiled a brand-new roller coaster system that seemed downright unthinkable: the inverted coaster. The prototype was dubbed *Batman—The Ride*, and it joined B&M's *Iron Wolf* at Six Flags Great America. When details of the attraction were first released, there was speculation that the ride just wouldn't work. As with the suspended coasters that came before it, its trains hung from an overhead track. But instead of free-swinging coaches, these vehicles were rigidly fixed to their wheel assemblies. This novel arrangement finally made possible the introduction of upside-down elements to the suspended coaster concept. History was in the making.

Batman—The Ride featured an ultra-tight layout, which included two vertical loops, a zero-G heartline spin, and a pair of corkscrews. But B&M pushed the thrill factor up yet another notch by making the vehicles resemble floorless ski lift–like cars, allowing riders' feet to dangle. This openness dramatically heightened the sense of flight. The world and the industry at large were justifiably amazed. To date, numerous examples of the successful *Batman—The Ride* have opened at Six Flags parks around the country (along with clones of the same design at other parks).

Bollinger & Mabillard went on to build even larger, more elaborate versions of this ride at parks around the world. North American installations that deserve mention include *Raptor* at Cedar Point, *Alpengeist* at Busch Gardens Williamsburg, *Montu* at Busch

Gardens Tampa Bay, and *Top Gun* at Paramount's Carowinds. These latter two inverted coasters are heavily themed and incorporate underground tunnels with fog and other special effects.

Other companies scrambled to hop on the inverted bandwagon, including the Dutch firm Vekoma, which went on to design the Suspended Looping Coaster (SLC). This affordable, compact ride featuring two-abreast seating began to show up at parks all over North America. This off-the-shelf production SLC sold as well as the firm's ultra-successful *Boomerang* shuttle loop popular in the 1980s. Vekoma even combined the two concepts and came out with the *Invertigo*, a suspended looping shuttle coaster.

In the meantime, B&M introduced a succession of larger standup and sit-down looping coasters. Each of these rides featured the now-familiar four-abreast seating and a degree of smoothness in the engineering process that was second to none. The firm entered the non-looping hyper-coaster market in 1999 with installations at Busch Gardens Williamsburg (*Apollo's Chariot*) and Six Flags Great America (*Raging Bull*).

In the late 1990s, other firms, including Morgan Manufacturing, Intamin, and Giavanola, joined the hypercoaster craze by building enormous non-looping steel coasters. Each of these wonderful rides was a success in its own right, but none seemed to equal the appeal of that very first hyper— Cedar Point's *Magnum XL200*. Even today, *Magnum* still ranks as one of the most popular steel roller coasters the world has ever seen, probably in part because of its magnificent lakeside setting.

LIM/LSM Power: Extreme Thrills

The traditional electrically driven chain lift is the method that most roller coasters employ to convey trains to the ride's highest section, of course. Typically, from that point on, the simple concept of gravity is all that's required to bring the trains back to the loading platform.

In 1976, a European conglomeration including Intamin, Schwarzkopf, and Reinhold Spieldiener came up with a mechanical linear accelerator, which they used as the launch device in their amazing shuttle loop coaster. This method was quite similar to the way jet aircraft are propelled off carriers at sea. But two decades later, a new propulsion system involving revolutionary electromagnetic linear accelerators came into

play in the entertainment sector following extensive experimentation in the passenger-train field, where the concept is known as "maglev," for magnetic levitation. Trains are essentially wheelless and float above the troughlike track through opposing polarities between track and train. The trains are propelled by electromagnetic impulses in the part of the track that surrounds the train.

Basically, two forms of this technology are currently in use on amusement rides: linear synchronous motors (LSM) and linear induction motors (LIM). Once the initial bugs were worked out, the latter method proved to be much more reliable and cost-effective. Intamin used LSMs to power its 100–MPH reverse free-fall rides: *Superman: The Escape* at Six Flags Magic Mountain and *Tower of Terror* at Australia's Dreamworld. Premier Rides of Millersville, Maryland, contracted with the United Kingdom's Force Engineering to provide LIM power for its line of high-tech looping steel roller coasters.

For example, aboard Six Flags' *Mr. Freeze*, *Poltergeist*, *Joker's Jinx*, or *Batman and Robin*, guests are catapulted out of the stations from 0 to 60 MPH in just over three seconds. Pulses of electromagnetic energy propel the heavy trains along a flat launch corridor and then shoot them to the ride's tallest point. From there, momentum produced by the launch and good old gravity provide the energy to return riders to the unloading platform.

The benefits of using linear-induction magnets in a roller coaster application are numerous: They basically eliminate space-consuming lift hills, have no moving parts which can wear out over time, and—once they are installed and calibrated—are virtually maintenance-free.

RIDE OF STEEL

Superman—Ride of Steel at New York's Six Flags Darien Lake was Intamin's first foray into the exclusive world of hypercoastering. Taking flight in 1999, *Superman* features an ultra steep 70-degree, 205-foot first drop into a sweeping turn inches above the surface the park's lake. Blistering speed and impressive airtime make this a must-ride. *Scott Rutherford*

Force Engineering provides a succinct explanation of just how its products produce power to propel roller coaster trains:

An LIM is fundamentally a rotating squirrel cage induction motor that has been opened flat. The magnetic field, instead of rotating, sweeps across the flat motor face. The stator, usually known as the LIM, consists of a three-phrase winding in a laminated iron core. When energized from an AC supply, a traveling wave magnetic field is produced. Travel can be reversed by swapping two phases. The reaction plate is the equivalent of the rotor. This is usually a conductor sheet of aluminum or copper backed by steel, but any of these may be used alone. Currents induced in the reaction plate by the stator traveling field create a secondary field.

In essence, a long series of LIMs are placed trackside along the level launch alley (or at other points along the course where the train might require a boost), just above the tubular rails. Long fins attached to the sides of the cars pass through the LIMs. The LIMs are powered in sequence, and the magnetic force generated pushes the train forward or in reverse.

On the Six Flags rides, 224 LIMs are generally required to launch the loaded trains into the heart of the coaster. The feeling is akin to being shot out of a cannon. Though LIMs require a large power supply and, according to some enthusiasts, rob the rider of the anticipation afforded by a slow, clanking chain lift, it seems this application of modern technology has been proven viable and will most likely show up on many amusement park rides in the future.

In 1996, two identical coaster systems were constructed using the available LIM technology. Designed by Germany's Werner Stengel and built by Premier Rides, these installations were called *The Outer Limits: Flight of Fear*. Simultaneously constructed at Paramount's Kings Dominion (Doswell, Virginia) and Paramount's Kings Island (Kings Island, Ohio), these rides were cleverly themed around the vintage 1960s TV show *The Outer Limits*. The completely enclosed coasters featured six-car trains being launched along a flat plane from 0 to 60 MPH in three seconds. At the end of the launch corridor, riders climbed the inside wall of the enclosure and were subjected to one of the tightest, most convoluted tangles of coaster track ever devised. Numerous inversions, severely banked turns, and compound curves produced a disorienting and turbulent tour of a darkened, planetarium-like building.

Several other incarnations of LIM-powered coasters followed, including the hyper-intense *Mr. Freeze* rides at Six Flags over Texas and Six Flags over St. Louis, and a pair of racing LIM coasters, *Batman and Robin: The Chiller* at Six Flags Great Adventure. Even Disney got in on the action in 1999, when it opened Vekoma's prototype LIM, *Rock-N-Roller Coaster* at the Disney MGM Studios. Numerous outdoor clones of the aforementioned *Outer Limits* subsequently were placed in operation at various parks in North America and abroad.

In 1998, Intamin married the LIM technology with the inverted coaster and built *Volcano: The Blast Coaster* at Paramount's Kings Dominion. This unusual ride involves riders seated in trains of ski lift–like vehicles which are blasted from 0 to 70 MPH in four seconds through a man-made mountain and then up through the lava vent of a simulated volcano. Though *V:TBC* has a relatively brief ride time, a series of smooth, graceful heartline spins around and finally back inside the mountain make it an intense and enjoyable experience. A larger, more elaborate version of this ride would be a wonderful addition to any park.

Though not a traditional roller coaster by any means, *Superman: The Escape* at Six Flags Magic Mountain deserves mention due to the sheer outrageousness of the ride experience. Utilizing LSM technology, a pair of 16-passenger vehicles on parallel tracks are launched from 0 to 100 MPH in six seconds. At the end of their level launch paths, the tracks arc 90 degrees upward and take riders 400 feet above the ground. Once they expend their energy, gravity takes over, and the cars free-fall back toward the ground and roll smoothly to a stop at their starting point. A single-track version of this amazing ride also opened at Australia's Dreamworld.

With this LIM/LSM method of propulsion at their disposal, steel-coaster designers are afforded virtually limitless possibilities. They can create layouts of practi-

cally any length or configuration without worrying about large, space-consuming lift hills. When their trains start to lose momentum, they simply pass them through a set of LIMs or LSMs and blast them merrily along their way.

Twenty-First Century Zaniness

As expected, the arrival of the New Age brings with it a number of rides which push the thrill envelope far beyond what anyone thought feasible or probable just a few years ago. There are three such coasters that fall into this over-the-top category.

Son of Beast, Paramount's Kings Island

Before Kings Island found itself under the stars of the Paramount banner, it became home to a legend called the *Beast*. In 1979, the park constructed the

MAGNETIC MAELSTROM

The *Mad Cobra* at Japan's Suzaka Circuitland opened in 1998 and was Premier Rides' 7th LIM "catapult coaster." The *Cobra* features trains launched from 0-60 MPH in about three seconds. The compact maze of track following the blast-off is loaded with inversions, banks, and compounds curves—intensity for the hardcore fan. *Gary Slade*

LOOPING DYNAMIC DUO

Six Flags Great Adventure took the LIM catapult-coaster concept and doubled the power for twice the fun. Heavily themed around Marvel Comics' Batman and Robin mythology, *The Chiller* offers parallel but radically different ride experiences. After the dramatic launch from the station, "Robin" (red) riders whip though a double-looping boomerang while the "Batman" train (blue) arcs into the taller "top hat" element. Then, both trains spin through twin heartline spins, climb a dead-end ramp, and are launched through the whole layout backward. *Scott Rutherford*

VOLCANO: THE BLAST COASTER

Paramount's Kings Dominion premiered this Intamin LIM suspended looping coaster in 1998. Integrated into a mountain facade, *Volcano: The Blast Coaster* uses four-car trains hanging from an overhead track that are launched out of the station and into the mountain. Additional LIMs then rocket riders vertically up and out of the lava vent. They emerge upside down and then begin a twisting, looping journey back to the loading platform. *Scott Rutherford*

longest wooden roller coaster humankind had ever attempted (outside of the Mauch Chunk Switch Back Railway outlined in chapter 1), and this pioneering theme park was again thrust into the limelight. And now, over two decades later, no other park has topped the *Beast's* claim to fame.

However, in the spring of 2000, the big daddy of wooden coasters will unleash his progeny upon an unsuspecting world. From initial impressions, this wicked kid just may give his famous father a run for his money. This outlandish effort, to be called *Son of Beast*, is the planet's tallest and fastest wooden roller coaster, and the only looping one. The terrain-driven ride stands 218 feet tall, sports 7,038 feet of laminated wooden track, and is spread over a hilly 12-acre site. Though the ride's two record-breaking drops of 214 and 164.11 feet and record speed of 78 MPH earn it top honors, its 103-foot-tall vertical loop really puts *Son of Beast* in a class by itself. Designed by German steel-coaster guru Werner Stengel for the Roller Coaster Corporation of America, *Son of Beast* may be an anomaly, but its extraordinary ride characteristics will most likely allow it retain its world records just as its father has. After all, who would even dare challenge this mighty pair?

Project Stealth, Paramount's Great America

The public loves something new and different. And when it's very, *very* different, people really stand up and take notice—or lie down, in the case of *Project Stealth*, the working name (as of this writing) of the new prototype coaster ringing in the twenty-first century at Paramount's Great America in Santa Clara, California.

Developed by Vekoma International of the Netherlands, this high-tech stomach churner combines the rush of hang-gliding with the controlled action of a steel looping coaster. As you might expect, park guests are clamoring for their chance to try it out. Flyers board six-car, 24-passenger trains and then secure harnesses about their knees and upper body. As the train departs the station and begins to ascend the 115-foot, 30-degree lift hill backwards, guests are slowly tilted to a prone position in their seats. With guests lying down, the train

then goes through the first inversion at the top of the hill so riders are suddenly flying face down toward the ground. Guests spend much the 50–MPH ride on their backs and fronts, whipping along 2,766 feet of coiling twists and turns.

According to park spokesman and those who have braved this unorthodox prototype ride, "It's a roller coaster all right, but you've never experienced anything like this before. Not anywhere. Not ever."

Millennium Force, Cedar Point

Considering the high-profile, one-of-a-kind ultra-thrillers opening in 2000, one might think Ohio's powerhouse themers, Cedar Point and Kings Island, are in some kind of personal coaster arms race. But they both insist that competition is healthy. So it's probably nothing more than a business decision that Cedar Point is gleefully shattering the current world record for the tallest and fastest roller coaster.

Appropriately dubbed *Millennium Force*, this steel super-hypercoaster arrives barely 10 years after Cedar

BEASTLY PREVIEW

This colorful cel from the Intraxx Corporation's *Son of Beast* pre-construction computer-generated animation shows an on-ride POV shot of what guests can expect when Paramount's Kings Island's record-breaking wooden roller coaster opens in 2000. This is the view from above the turn off the lift hill, heading toward the ride's perilous 218-foot first drop. The monstrous vertical loop dominating this shot will be the first such upside-down element ever attempted on a modern wooden coaster. *Intraxx*

COASTER DESIGN AND ENGINEERING
A New-Age Approach

LIGHTNING RACER, HERSHEYPARK

An animation cell depicting the incredible new *Lightning Racer* set to open at Hersheypark in 2000. The ride is yet another retro-classic from Great Coasters International. *INTRAX*

Marketing amusement rides in the new millennium takes more than words and static pictures. The MTV-and-video-game culture demands complicated animations long before a ride is ever built. INTRAXX Corporation of Lexington, Ohio, fills this demand with technically accurate and highly visual computer-generated animations.

INTRAXX was founded in 1993 by Frank and Teresa Purtiman. After concentrating on architectural models, they began producing computer-generated animations in 1996. Their clients include amusement parks such as Cedar Point, Paramount's Kings Island, Hersheypark, and those under the Six Flags banner, plus manufacturers such as Custom Coasters International.

INTRAXX has written proprietary software that works in conjunction with commercially available animation packages to recreate nearly the exact speed and timing of a particular roller coaster ride. From the lift hill to the brake run, INTRAXX prides itself on its ability to animate coasters at their correct velocities throughout the ride. In addition, the attention paid to the details of vehicle movement also allows parks and manufacturers to see exactly how a ride will perform long before even the first test runs are taken.

INTRAXX also pays great attention to ride and environmental details. Structure, trains, ride accessories, and even landscape can be detailed down to the smallest bolt and blade of grass using CAD (computer-aided design) files and topography information. INTRAXX used these techniques successfully for an animation of *Millennium Force*, Cedar Point's record-breaking hypercoaster. This project required INTRAXX to recreate the area's islands and peninsulas, as well as Lake Erie so the client could see how the ride would fit into the park environment.

After specializing in amusement rides for many years, INTRAXX has developed the ability to animate nearly any type of ride with little to no CAD data available. Frank Purtiman, president and CEO of INTRAXX, learned to recreate the specific designs of a coaster in CAD in order to have the necessary tools for animating the ride.

"Without our extensive background in amusement engineering and design, we could not have achieved the degree of smoothness and detail that we have created on many of our animations," Frank comments.

Using storyboards jointly created by INTRAXX and the client, each animation is designed around the specific marketing strategy of the park or manufacturer. "Manufacturers often try to highlight the engineering details of the ride," states INTRAXX Vice President Teresa Purtiman. "Their focus is usually on details that accentuate their unique designs and manufacturing, such as special track designs." Parks, on the other hand, often concentrate on the environment surrounding the ride.

An additional feature that INTRAXX has begun including with its animations is compressed quicktime movies of the animation for web publication. "Most parks and many manufacturers now have websites that are visited by thousands of their customers every year," Teresa comments. "By providing our clients with animations suitable for publication on the web, we open up a whole new customer segment for the client's animation."

Samples of this fascinating new technology designed specifically to generate computer imagery of roller coasters can be found on the INTRAXX website: www.intraxx.com

Point took the industry by storm with the introduction of *Magnum XL200*, the first hypercoaster. And like Madonna, Cedar Point is reinventing itself again by raising the stakes—to over 300 feet this time.

Millennium Force, designed by Werner Stengel for Intamin, sports a lift hill of a record 310 feet and a 300-foot first drop (also a record) angled at a horrific 80 degrees. With 6,595 feet of tubular steel track, *Millennium Force* features no conventional inversions but will instead have curves over-banked at 122 degrees. So although the three trains will not actually travel upside down, they will be tilted well past horizontal during certain points of the ride to compensate for the excessive speed. Besides its colossal rate of travel, the sweeping course contains tunnels and a collection of drops and turns that guarantee you'll never forget *Millennium Force*

Don't get let your guard down quite yet, though. This coaster war is hardly over. A larger steel coaster from an Morgan Manufacturing under construction for Japan's Nagashima Spaland, and it promises to eclipse even Cedar Point's newest surreal monstrosity. In the summer of 2000, the as-yet-unnamed ride will become the world's tallest (more than 300 feet), fastest (more than 90 MPH), and longest (more than 8,000 feet) roller coaster.

Wooden Coasters Come Full Circle

As we bid farewell to the twentieth century, one might be inclined to think that steel roller coasters standing over 30 stories high and their cousins capable of performing outlandish aerial antics would have quickly replaced their old-fashioned wooden counterparts. Thankfully, though, the situation is actually quite the opposite.

It is often said that history repeats itself. When applying that old adage to the resurgence of interest in the unique experience of riding the wooden roller coaster, this appears readily apparent. The wooden coaster's popularity has been on a constant upswing since the opening of the Kings Island *Racer* back in 1972. Though the industry did suffer the loss of hundreds of classic rides from the 1930s through the early 1970s, now the renewed interest in the wooden roller coaster continues to grow with each passing season.

Modern companies like Custom Coasters International, Great Coasters International, and Roller Coaster Corporation of America have refined the art of wooden coaster design and construction to such a degree that this traditional ride is once again an integral and necessary facet of today's amusement park experience. These old standbys are now as popular and well-loved as their towering steel brethren, and in many cases, even more so. It appears that perhaps, at least in the amusement arena, we as a culture are finally realizing that we *can* learn a thing or two from our rich and vibrant history, that valuable knowledge lies in the past, just waiting to be recognized and incorporated into the rides of today.

Wooden coaster manufacturers and park owners are finally realizing that bigger coasters are not necessarily better coasters. Maintaining a large wooden ride is extremely costly. Wood, being organic and supple, can only take so much punishment before requiring replacement. The laminated wooden rails on the mammoth wooden coasters built during the late 1980s and early 1990s have worn out much faster than on older coasters due to the combination of stress, weight, and higher speeds. Because of their sheer enormity, many of those large wooden rides have been re-profiled and tamed with braking to slow the wear and tear caused by the magnified forces. The general result of this butchering is a large but frankly mundane coaster. And it is a known fact that an attraction unpopular with the general public is not a marketable product.

THRUST AIR 2000

Developed by S&S Power, Inc., the *Thrust Air 2000* is an extreme ride which leave riders giddy and spectators shaking their heads in disbelief. This amazing machine utilizes compressed air pressure to launch its single vehicle out of the station at 80 MPH and up a vertical climb of 172 feet angled at 90 degrees. Once over the top, riders plummet straight back to the ground, pulling out of the dive at the last second. The photo shows the ride during its 1999 media preview at the Utah factory. *Gary Slade*

Medium Is a Rare and Wonderful Thing

Enter the era of the medium-sized coaster. Today, modern wooden-coaster designers have learned that rides in the 80- to 100-foot-high range are the way to go for a variety of reasons. These machines cost far less to build and maintain than some gargantuan, over-built mutants erected merely to shatter another park's usually short-lived world record. And strange as it might seem, many of these medium-sized coasters are fundamentally more entertaining to ride.

A quick look back through history reveals that some of the greatest wooden coasters ever built fell into this category. Playland Park's *Airplane*, the Idora *Wildcat*, the Riverview *Bobs*, and countless others would today be considered medium-sized rides. Even the incomparable Coney Island *Cyclone*, the most famous pre-Depression wooden roller coaster still in operation, stands a mere 85 feet tall. And though the *Cyclone* has been around for over 70 years, it remains one of the best on the planet and still draws large crowds.

Golden-age designers instinctively knew that a good ride was as contrived as a riveting novel and as cleverly choreographed as classic ballet. These talented gentlemen orchestrated each project to be an all-out assault on the senses. Instead of building towering monuments to excess, they instilled their creations with that all-important and necessary ingredient called *"action."* They crammed as much as they possibly could into compact packages, overlapping and layering trackage, stacking and nesting turns, and adding a slew of other subtle but effective nuances. These space-saving building techniques visually heightened the thrill factor. A by-product of trains flying through these forests of timber and crossbeams was an enhanced sense of speed. These pioneers filled their rides with surprise after surprise, never giving riders a chance to catch their breaths or regain their composure until they reached the safety of the unloading platform. When you disembarked, weak-kneed and wobbly, from one of these golden-age thrillers, you knew you'd been on a roller coaster. It was pure showmanship, all carefully blended into a kinetic frenzy of roaring, rattling motion, a body-wrenching emotional experience with which nothing on earth could compare.

Fortunately for those who crave the old-fashioned feel of a traditional wooden roller coaster, designers and builders like Michael Boodley and Clair Hain Jr. of Great Coasters International, as well as the crew at Custom Coasters International, among others, are resurrecting a part of the past for future generations to enjoy.

So, even though there will continue to be new and innovative steel rides sprouting up all over the world, the old-fashioned wooden roller coaster continues to hold its own as the true king of the midway. And thanks to modern designer firms like GCI, CCI, and their colleagues, the indomitable spirit of those pioneers of the first golden age will live on and prosper well into the new millennium.

HERSHEYPARK *WILDCAT*

The beautiful *Wildcat* at Pennsylvania's Hersheypark was Great Coasters International's debut effort. Opened in 1996, this supertwister was directly inspired by the wooden wonders built by Fred Church and other masters from the roller coaster's first golden age. With a height of around 100 feet and turns which seem to never end, GCI proves that a coaster doesn't have to be the biggest to be the best. Creativity and hidden surprises make the *Wildcat* a Hersheypark's to ride, again and again. *Scott Rutherford*

Glossary

Airtime: The sensation of floating during low- or negative-gravity moments. These instances of weightlessness are found over the tops of low-lying "speed hills" or during abrupt downward and upward transitions. Airtime is considered by coaster fans to be an extremely important ingredient for a good roller coaster.

Banked turn: A curve in which the track is significantly angled to reduce stress on riders and withstand the thrust of the train as it negotiates the turn.

Bat wing: This maneuver is a variation of the boomerang. Found mainly on inverted (hanging) coasters, it is a double-looping element, the center portion of which is usually low to the ground.

Boomerang: Also know as a "cobra roll," this popular element is found on looping steel coasters. It consists of a twisted double-inversion in which the train enters the element, flips over twice, and exits in the opposite, though parallel, direction. Also the name for a standard type of steel shuttle coaster produced by Vekoma of the Netherlands.

Corkscrew: A single, double, or triple helix found on steel looping coasters. Also the name for a standard type of steel roller coaster produced by Arrow Dynamics.

Dark ride: An amusement attraction in which much of the total ride time is spent indoors, taking riders past fun house—like stunts and other surprises. Some of the later *Scenic Railways* (and even several modern coasters) featured enclosed/dark track areas.

Double dip: Usually found on wooden coasters, the double dip can be an airtime producer if it is designed correctly. Basically, the track drops halfway down, levels out, and then plunges to the ground. The best example of a double dip that truly works is on Kennywood Park's *Jack Rabbit*. Some coasters also feature a double up.

Fan turn: A 180-degree turn of roller coaster track raised up at an angle. Sometimes half fan turns can be found, but both usually produce impressive lateral forces as trains careen around them and slam riders into the car sides.

Flat turn: As opposed to the fan or swoop turn, flat turns are long, wide-radius sections of track that are modestly banked. Though usually unexciting, if taken at high speeds, these flat turns can induce a rollicking ride due to their lateral G forces.

Footprint: The shape of a roller coaster's overall layout and the acreage it occupies.

G force: Gravitational forces, either negative or positive, exerted on riders by the motion of the trains as they speed along the layout.

Helix: A section of track that circles upon itself at least once, either ascending or descending in the process.

Hypercoaster: A term coined in 1989 when Cedar Point opened its *Magnum XL200*. A hypercoaster features a lift hill and/or drop of 200 feet or more.

Inversion: A ride element that turns riders upside down in one manner or another with vertical loops, corkscrews, or other gyrations.

Inverted coaster: A close cousin to the suspended coaster, an inverted coaster's track is—like that of the suspended coaster—above the train, but the cars are rigidly attached to the wheels and do not swing.

Lap bar: A style of restraint that is lowered by a ride attendant across the laps of guests to protect them during the coaster's turbulent journey.

Lift hill (also chain lift): A hill up which coaster cars or trains are hauled, usually via motorized drag chain. It is typically, but not always, the first and highest hill on a coaster. A single ride may have more than one lift hill.

NAD: National Amusement Device, Inc., a wooden roller coaster design and building firm active between the 1930s and 1960s. This firm built several notable coasters, including the Rockaway's Playland *Atom Smasher* and the surviving Mexico City racing coaster. NAD's greatest contribution was the introduction of the Century Flyer, art deco-inspired rolling stock.

Out-and-back: A coaster with a simple layout in which the track heads more or less straight out to its far end, turns, and sprints back to the station. This type of coaster is usually milder and faster than a twister or ravine ride.

PTC: Philadelphia Toboggan Company (now Philadelphia Toboggan Coasters). One of the most famous and prolific wooden-coaster designers and builders. Today the company supplies most of the coaster trains for the world's wooden coasters and is now also offering steel-coaster trains.

Racing coaster: A coaster system featuring one or more trains traveling on adjacent runs of track. Parallel tracks of contemporary racing coasters are designed to operate as separate entities, though it was popular with pioneering designers to fashion the course as one long interconnected circuit—the train that departed the station on the left side would return to the right side upon completing its run.

Scenic railway: A mild-mannered roller coaster made popular in the early 1900s. The ride often featured a themed environment both indoors and out. Many scenic railways were actually named *Scenic Railway*.

Shuttle loop: A point-to-point steel coaster in which the train is launched through one or more looping elements both forward and backward.

Side-friction coaster: Wooden coasters which utilize a channel-like track in which vertical running boards are used to keep the car—equipped with side-friction wheels—on course.

Single-seat articulated train: A train comprised of a four-wheeled pilot car and a series of two-wheeled single-seat coaches (typically holding two riders) that are hitched like trailers behind one another. This arrangement allows the cars' wheels to bear evenly upon the rails at all times, ensuring a smooth ride and excellent tracking. Most modern steel coasters feature this arrangement.

Speed bump: A low-lying hill following a larger drop that usually causes riders to float out of their seats.

Standup coaster: A coaster which has trains without seats or sides. Instead, riders stand, straddling a bicycle-like seat, within special restraints anchored to the floor of the cars. There are no sides to the cars per se, so the rider feels complete openness.

Suspended coaster: A coaster featuring trains that hang below their track on wheel assemblies. A hinge arrangement allows the cars to swing out on the curves. Since the overhead track is not prominently visible to riders, a suspended coaster simulates the sensation of acrobatic flying.

Terrain (gully or ravine) coaster: A coaster that uses undulating or irregular topography to its advantage. By utilizing ravines and valleys, drops can be made longer and more surprising with less support structure.

Tubular steel-track coaster: A track fabrication format developed in the late 1950s in which the rails consist entirely of hollow steel tubing, with welded steel rail spacers (ties).

Twister: A coaster with a convoluted track configuration in which the layout twists continuously over, under, and back on itself.

Upstop wheels: Also known as under-friction wheels, this revolutionary safety device was developed by coaster pioneer John Miller at the beginning of the twentieth century. These crucial components of a coaster car's wheel assembly are positioned beneath a ride's running rails. They effectively keep the vehicle locked to the track and prevented upward movement and derailing. Upstop wheels are paramount on rides that feature strong low-G moments or upside-down elements.

Wood-track coaster: Traditional coaster track construction featuring laminated wooden planks (usually around nine-ply) on which steel running rails and side-friction rails are bolted. Steel weight-bearing wheels, side wheels, and upstop wheels hug the top and insides of the laminated wood track assembly and keep the coaster train safely on course as it hurtles along.

Index